PRAI[illegible]

My Future's So Bright

"I just finished Trina Boice's book *My Future's So Bright, I Gotta Wear Shades!* Trina has done an amazing job of mixing humor, logic, and the teachings of modern day prophets to make this book both appealing and valuable. I highly recommend this book to both the youth and their parents. It will be a tremendous benefit to those who will read and follow the principles shared."

—**Randal Wright**, author of *Power Parenting in the LDS Home* and *Helping Youth Stay Morally Clean*

"Trina Boice provides a wonderful and lighthearted way for teens to see those things in their life that can cloud their vision of eternal things. Easy to read and filled with fun illustrations, kids will find themselves smiling as they begin to see themselves through different lenses. This book comes at a critical time as LDS youth are being challenged as never before. It helps them better understand the joy they will feel as they proudly stand for what they believe. As they begin to 'see as they are seen,' they will better understand their place in the plan of happiness. A must read for today's amazing youth!"

—**Kevin Hinkley**, M.Ed LPC, author of *Habits, Hurts, and Hangups: 12 Steps to Heal the Natural Man* and *The Husband Whisperer: The Gentle Approach to Communication in Marriage*

My Future's SO BRIGHT, I GOTTA WEAR SHADES

TRINA BOICE

CFI
An imprint of Cedar Fort, Inc.
Springville, Utah

This is not an official publication of The Church of Jesus Christ of Latter-day Saints. The opinions and views expressed herein belong solely to the authors and do not necessarily represent the opinions or views of Cedar Fort, Inc. Permission for the use of sources, graphics, and photos is also solely the responsibility of the authors.

ISBN 13: 978-1-4621-1417-7

Published by CFI, an imprint of Cedar Fort, Inc.
2373 W. 700 S., Springville, UT 84663
Distributed by Cedar Fort, Inc., www.cedarfort.com

LIBRARY OF CONGRESS CATALOGING-IN-PUBLICATION DATA

Boice, Trina, 1963- author.
My future's so bright, I gotta wear shades! / Trina Boice.
pages cm
Includes bibliographical references and index.
ISBN 978-1-4621-1417-7 (alk. paper)
1. Mormon youth--Conduct of life. 2. Mormon youth--Religious life. 3. Church of Jesus Christ of Latter-day Saints--Doctrines. 4. Mormon Church--Doctrines. I. Title.

BX8643.Y6B65 2014
248.8'3--dc23

2014017505

Cover design by Shawnda T. Craig

Edited and typeset by Jessica B. Ellingson

Printed in the United States of America

10 9 8 7 6 5 4 3 2 1

Printed on acid-free paper

Dedication

This book is dedicated to all of the teenagers in my family: my four amazing sons, who put up with me every day (Cooper, Calvin, Brad, Bo); and my wonderful nieces and nephews, who make me so proud of their talents, accomplishments and valiant testimonies (Steven, Misha, Brittany, Tanner, Lacey, Tyler, Bridgette, and Ben).

When these kids were little, other parents would shake their heads in pity and say with sad voices of warning, "Wow, just wait until they're all crazy teenagers!" We had fun when they were young, but we *love* having crazy teenagers! They make me laugh all the time and I'm so grateful that we get to share our journey through life together!

Other Books by Trina Boice

- *Dad's Night: Fantastic Family Nights in 5 Minutes*
- *Ready Resource for Relief Society* volumes 1–4
- *Sabbath Solutions: More Than 350 Ways You Can Worship on the Lord's Day*
- *Easy Enrichment Ideas: Thinking Outside the Green Gelatin Box*
- *Climbing Family Trees: Whispers in the Leaves*
- *Bright Ideas for Young Women Leaders*
- *Great Ideas for Primary Activity Days*
- *Parties With A Purpose: Exciting Ideas for Ward Activities*
- *Primarily For Cub Scouts*
- *How to Stay UP in a DOWN Economy*
- *103 Creative Ways to Announce Your Pregnancy*
- *A Gift of Love*

Contents

Acknowledgments

It takes a lot of people to put a great book together! Did I just say this book is great? Well, yeah! And I'm not the least bit biased! Okay, maybe just a little. When you're finished reading, I hope you'll say the same thing. (The part about it being great, not biased.)

I want to thank my family for always being so supportive of my projects and passions. It has been a humbling honor to raise four amazing sons: Cooper, Calvin, Brad, and Bo. I'd love to think that I taught them a lot, but they were the ones who taught me how to raise kids and gave me the gift of being a mom.

I would also like to thank everyone at Cedar Fort who worked tirelessly on this fun book with me: Jessica Ellingson, Emily Chambers, Shawnda Craig, Heather Holm, and Kelly Martinez.

A special thanks goes to some very special teenagers who read the book, offered edits, and gave me the thumbs up or thumbs down as they read: my lovely and accomplished niece, Misha Duncan, and her dearest friend, Elisa Huhem, whose picture is all over the BeSmart and BYU websites! My incredibly talented niece, Brittany Long, is a professional editor who also created the magical comics throughout the book.

I also want to thank this entire generation of LDS teens who are responding so eagerly to the Lord's hastening of missionary work. It brings me to tears every time I see one of them jump at the opportunity to serve a full-time mission and represent the Lord far away from their friends and family. What a privilege it is to rub shoulders with these truly valiant Latter-day Saints. You inspire me every day!

Each chapter includes advice from friends who graciously accepted my request to share their wisdom: Janice Kapp Perry, Steven Sharp Nelson, Jordan Bluth, Josi Kilpack, Michael Young, Audrey Denison, Jenny Jordan Frogley, Peter Hollens, Jessie Funk, Nichole Giles, Dawn Norton, Marsha Ward, Lindsey Stirling, Deirdra Eden, Annette Luthy Lyon, Tristi Pinkston, Rebecca Cornish Talley, Cameron C. Taylor, Crista Guthrie, Fay Klingler, Natalee Lence, Janet Kay Jensen, Ronda Hinrichsen, Jason Mchood Hansen, Tracey Long, Brad Boice, Nathan Grant, Sheila Windley Staley, Antonio Roman Reyna, Mike Coombs, Brian Kehoe, Suzanne Jason

Acknowledgments

Love, Karen McLennan, J. Andrews, Tom Tam, Ryan Rose Weaver, Susan Horrocks, Richard Maycock, Nick Giordano, Catherine Reese Newton, Brenda Brockly Boissevain, Mary Canale Sanders, Tera Duncan, Scott Galet, Lucas Worthen, Stephanie Stewart, Roger Hayes, Lisa Brereton, Tannar Manuirirangi, Steven Duncan, Keaton Hawker, Alexandria Clawson, Tanner Long, Elizabeth Thompson, Gracie Platt, Michael Grogitsky, Mason Parkes, Benny Yamagata, Chris Monahan, Kathleen Larkin Wardle, Jennifer Jackson, Sheila Windley Staley, Susan L. Corpany, Kevin Johnson, Leslie Gansel Bauscher, Jonathan Kaplan, Sean Flemming, Paula Flatman, Lori Jones, Steven Kendrick, Gina Nielsen, Barbara Smith Bailes, Sheila Whittaker, Traci Schull Heppler, Jennifer Smith El Alami, Rosshanti Caslol, Alex Rice, Richard Fritzler, Jennifer Meuter Parry, Chris Jensen, Sandra Brazner Meek, Gene Sasville, Harry Wood, Nathan Lurie, Adam Draper, Hailey Sheridan, Karen Oliver Sampson, Cheri Crane, Paula Rice Rogers, Shara Edwards. Thank you all!

CHAPTER ONE

How Do You SEE the World?

Hey, before I say anything, I just want to tell you how awesome I think you are! I mean, you're reading a "churchy" book in your spare time! You rock.

So, do you want to know how to look cool in three seconds? Put on a pair of dark sunglasses. Instant coolness factor. It's true. Do you want to know how to see better? Put on your eternal-vision glasses. How do you do that? Look past today and think about where you're going to spend your future.

How you look at the world can determine how you behave. Perspective is how we see things from where we are in our lives. Our perspective may change, depending upon our experiences and circumstances. What perspective of the world around you do *you* have? How do you see your life? Is it really how the world is or just how you *think* it is?

In this book you're going to read about some things that might make you look at the world and your life in a new way. All of the experiences you've had in your life have been shaping how you relate to the world and others, and how you interpret things. It's enlightening to realize that others see us based on their past experiences with people similar to us, as well as everything that has trained them to interpret the world in a certain way.

FUN NEWS

One of my friends and I made an app just for you! And it's free! Woohoo! (Free is my jam!) Upload a picture of your face and you get to play around with a bunch of different sunglasses. Kinda fun, right? Find it on my website at www.trinaboice.com.

Imagine looking out a perfectly clean, clear window. You see the world as it is. Now imagine that someone splashed mud on the window. A bug is splattered on the corner pane. Yuck. A neighborhood kid with terrible aim threw a ball and chipped part of the glass. Now add years of snowstorms, wind, and sun damage. How is your view out of that window now? How does the world look?

How Do You SEE the World?

Each of those things represents your life's experiences and how they might change your view on the world—good and bad. If your parents got a divorce or you won the lottery or you were born into a family as the only child or you lived with your grandparents who smoked—all of those things give you experience that influence how you look at the world and other people. A simple change in your life or your very own attitude can alter how you **SEE**.

We're also going to talk about a place where you are going to spend a lot of time . . . your future! The future can be twenty-five years from now, twenty-five minutes from now, or even twenty-five seconds from right now. Eternity has already begun. Have you ever thought that today is part of your eternity? The choices you're making today and how you are choosing to live your life will determine where you will spend your future! The Young Women's value "Choice and Accountability" is an important reminder that our choices every day truly determine the *quality* of our lives.

In your parents' language, the word *future* usually means college, mission, marriage, career, and grandchildren. When they talk to you about your future, it may sound like they're speaking a foreign language at times. They tend to focus their lectures on your future safety, security, and responsibility. Teenagers, on the other hand, often define the word *future* as next Friday night's dance. Teens tend to focus their energies on fun, friendship, and freedom. There's nothing wrong with those things when placed among other items that will actually prepare you for events past next Friday night's dance.

If you can understand your parents' goals for you and know that they have those goals because they have lived through a few Friday night dances themselves and have a larger perspective now, then you'll actually appreciate the advice they're trying to give. (Heads up: the word "*advice*" is a parent code word for *lecture*.) Once they see your appreciation for their good intentions they *will* get off your back more! Tell them, "Hey, thanks for your advice!" and I promise you'll get to that Friday night dance faster.

TIP FOR GETTING ALONG WITH YOUR PARENTS

Instead of rolling your eyes at their lectures, thank your parents and ask them questions. Crazy, right? They'll think you're the most magnificent teenager in the world. Oh yeah, you are.

President Spencer W. Kimball gave an excellent talk to teenagers entitled "Planning Your Life." In it he says, "You are maturing and assuming responsibility. The most important decisions of your entire life are before you—decisions which can open up for your future glorious, progressive pathways" (*New Era*, Sept. 1981, 47).

Now is the time to put on your "big kid" pants and be a part of the world! You have some exciting decisions to make in the next few years, decisions that will affect the quality of your entire life. It's a little bit scary to transition from a carefree kid to a responsible adult. Thankfully, you get to practice one day at a time and you won't be expected to jump from playing Mario Brothers to filling out tax forms all in one day.

One important point to remember is that while you have the freedom to make your own choices, you do not have the power to choose the consequences

saturday 08 february

GROWN-UP THINGS I DID TODAY:

- clean the kitchen
- mop the floor
- work on commission
- finish a Jane Austen novel
- watch a Regency-era film
- blog

KID THINGS I DID TODAY:

- eat chocolate chip pancakes for breakfast
- make a blanket fort with lil' sister
- put each of the puppies through coat sleeves & die laughing while they try to get out
- have chips for lunch

of your choices. When you make a choice, you are inevitably choosing the consequence that naturally follows that decision. For example, if you choose to smoke, you are also choosing to have health problems, social stigma, financial loss, and often punishment from your parents once they find out! On the other hand, if you choose a college education, you are also choosing improved income, enhanced self-esteem, respect, new friendships, broader experiences, and the chance to open more doors to your future. *The consequences that are automatically tied to your choices are both earthly and eternal.*

President Gordon B. Hinckley said, "You are creatures of divinity; you are daughters [and sons] of the Almighty. Limitless is your potential. Magnificent is your future, *if you will take control of it.*" ("How Can I Become the Woman of Whom I Dream?" *Ensign*, May 2001; emphasis added).

RANDOM THOUGHT ABOUT PROPHETS

President Hinckley's doctor told him he needed to be careful walking as he got older and so he gave him a cane to carry. President Hinckley literally *carried* it and used it as a poker and pointer rather than use it for walking. He even used it to resemble a sword and dubbed Elder Eyring a pretend knight with it! I loved how President Hinckley always had a bright smile, even when the world was turning dark around us. I think it was because he knew how the story is going to end.

In a talk to the youth, President Hinckley spoke about an old yearbook and the memories it flashed in his mind. Older people are always amazed at how quickly the years have flown by. I'm not super old yet, but I've been doing a lot of thinking about the past lately too, especially my high school years. I was the senior class president in my high school and am now planning my thirty-year high school reunion. EEK! That makes me sound so old! There is no way I graduated from high school thirty years ago, but that's what the calendar on my wall says. It feels like just yesterday when I was hanging out with my friends at lunchtime on campus, but it also feels like another life-time ago. I still feel like a young teenager inside, but the mirror says otherwise. I also feel more experienced and wise than I was back then. I definitely have a tougher time staying up past midnight on Friday nights than I did when I was a teenager! Yikes! I *am* old!

As part of the high school reunion event, we're putting together a "Biography Book" that will be copied and distributed to all of the classmates. We each have to write a "bio" page that highlights how we have spent the last thirty years. We can include photos, quotes, or whatever we choose to represent our lives. It's hard to condense thirty years of life's experiences on to an 8 ½ X 11 page of blank paper! What have my classmates done with their lives? What can I say I've done with mine?

How about you? What do you want to say you did with your life thirty years from now? I know that feels like an eternity away from today. Think about writing a page like that now. "How?" you ask. Simply decide what you want to happen in your future. Of course, we can't completely control what will be in our future, but you can make plans for things you would like to happen. Some people call it a "Bucket List." You know, things you want to accomplish in your life before you "kick the bucket."

Fill this out right now. What do you want to . . .

Be:

Do:

Have:

Give:

The Lord may have many surprises in store for you, but what we're going to talk about in this book are all of the things you really *can* control in your future! Decide what kind of life you want to have ten years from now . . . or thirty . . . or fifty . . . or more! What will the quality of your life be? What aspects of a good, happy, successful life will you include? College degrees? Temple marriage? Mission? Children? World travel? Community service? Political aspirations? The possibilities are limitless!

Of course, you hope to be a big success, but what exactly is success? Decide now how *you* define that word and what you need to do to attain it. Your future is *your* choice!

I asked a bunch of my friends (adults and teenagers) to share their best tips on how to be successful and happy in life. You'll see their advice at the end of each chapter. Here are a few tips to get you thinking.

SUCCESS TIPS FROM MY WISE FRIENDS

- The biggest key to happiness is to have a vision for your life. No matter how young or old you are, have the courage to walk away from anyone or anything that holds you back from what you are capable of doing. —Audrey Denison (She was Miss Teen Nevada in 2010! She is a recent convert with an awesome conversion story I'll share with you someday. She is currently serving a full-time mission in Washington, Vancouver!)
- If you *want* to be successful, you can and will be successful. —Jason McHood Hansen
- The secret of happiness is to make others believe they are the cause of it. —Mike Coombs
- Follow your heart. —Brian Kehoe
- If someone tells you that you can't, keep going until you find someone who says you can. —Suzanne Jasons Love

You decide where you will spend the future. Sure, there are circumstances in your life now that can help or hinder your progress toward certain goals, but if you plan now and work hard, it can happen!

Have you noticed that this book is full of words about glasses? Prophets and apostles are called **SEERS**. Listening to their counsel can help you shape your future into something great! Today *you* can decide what you will **SEE** in your future by the choices you make. How do you **SEE** your life now and in the future? Guess what? Your future is *so* bright! You better put some shades on!

By the way, this book is meant be a workbook that you can write in to help plan your future. Yes, I give you permission to write on the pages!

Write down some decisions you need to make this week about . . .

School:

Work:

Family:

Church:

Talents:

Health:

Now, list the big decisions you need to make within the next year or two.

Dating:

College:

Career:

Mission:

Marriage:

Health:

Church calling:

Talents:

RANDOM JOKE ABOUT GLASSES

A policeman stops a lady and asks for her license.
Policeman: "Lady, it says here that you should be wearing glasses."
Woman: "Well, I have contacts."
Policeman: "I don't care who you know! You're still getting a ticket!"

CHAPTER TWO

Nerd Glasses: Embrace the Awkward!

By now you've probably discovered that we Mormons are pretty weird. The scriptures actually call us a "peculiar people." (Do a word search on lds.org and you'll see not one, but six different scripture references when God lovingly refers to us as peculiar!) Embrace the awkward! Considering the world adores what's raunchy and evil and even warped, it's a good thing to be different from the world.

Yeah, we live "in" the world, but we don't have to be "of" it. Game on!

I love watching silly sitcoms on TV, but it's getting harder and harder to find ones that aren't complete trash. For example, sitcoms show couples sleeping and living together before marriage as if it's completely normal. They never show the consequences of such a lifestyle: unwanted pregnancies, sexually transmitted diseases, broken hearts, destroyed families, and on and on. The truth is that there *are* consequences.

I had a blast in high school, but I also felt ready to move on long before my graduation. Everyone seemed so immature. I was tired of the cliques, the judging, the parties where my friends got drunk, and watching my friends make really stupid choices. I kind of felt like I had outgrown them. Do you ever feel that way?

Here's the thing though: there *are* some hidden gems in your school. Find them. They're often the less popular kids who are quietly observing everything and everyone, learning from others' mistakes, and developing talents that will later make them shine. They're often the wallflowers who bloom later. They're the ones who genuinely get excited about learning and new ideas. They're the ones who are thinking, planning, and preparing for the future. In a nutshell, they're super interesting! You might even be one of them.

You may be envious of some of those popular kids who seem to be having all of the fun. Sadly, for some of them, this is the best part of their lives. It all goes down hill from here. Now, that's not true for all of them, of course. The gems will stand out as being authentic and real, not phony and fake. That's one sure sign. Look for those kids. If they're the real deal, they'll gladly welcome you into their circle of friendship. They'll recognize that *you* are a gem too!

Write a list of people you'd like to get to know better who might be gems.

*

*

*

My parents are party animals, so when we moved into a new house and school in eighth grade, they wanted my twin sister and me to throw a big party at our house to get to know people. We were excited and invited as many people as we knew. Twins are pretty noticeable, so word got out that "the twins" were throwing a party and a ton of people showed up. I'm all for big parties, and I was thrilled to fill the house with new friends.

One of the guys who came to the house had a reputation of being a "real" partier, as in "Party hard, dude!" He was cool and popular, so I wanted him to stay. You know, to increase the coolness factor of the event. "Where's the kegger, man?" he asked as he took one look around and realized it wasn't going to be one of "those" parties. I joked about the punch and cookies on the table, which were included in our innocent spread, and somehow I convinced him to stay. It was a fun night, and he and I became buds.

Jump ahead five years to our high school graduation. We had stayed friends during all of those tumultuous teen years, even though he kept up his serious party boy rep. After the graduation ceremony, he came up to me and asked, "You know what the best party I ever went to was?" I shrugged and replied, "I don't know, Dude . . . You went to a *lot* of parties!" He laughed and then suddenly got serious. He said, "Remember that sweet party you hosted at your house when we were just kids in eighth grade?" I was surprised he even remembered. In fact, I joked and told him that it was probably his favorite because he was usually so drunk at all of the other parties that mine was probably the only one he *did* remember! He agreed, but said, "Nah, yours was just really fun." It may have been the only party he ever attended where people weren't getting drunk or stoned. Instead, we had played games, danced, laughed, and had good, clean fun. That really made an impression on him.

You want to know what's funny? He owns a bar now! He and I still keep in touch. If he's ever finally ready to accept the gospel, he'll remember how much fun Mormon parties can be. Be brave, invite people over, and show them how to have "good" fun, and dare I say . . . peculiar fun?

What fun events do you have to look forward to in your bright future?

- New Year's Eve youth dances
- Prom and the Mormon "Formal" if you have one of those in your stake
- Homecoming float-making parties
- Grad night
- High school reunions
- Weddings
- Mission Farewells and Homecoming Open House gatherings
- Family reunions
- Baby showers
- Bridal showers
- Any time there is a reason to celebrate and be together!

My sisters and I are currently raising teenagers who are going through that same awkward stage that you are. We constantly encourage them to invite people over and throw parties so they can get to know people, develop social skills, and create fun memories and lasting friendships. In fact, we even wrote a book filled with party game ideas to help them be awesome hosts! They've helped test out our ideas, so only the ones that were approved by them as not being completely lame have made it into the book. Be sure to download it when it's offered for free as an ebook on Amazon! It's called "Creative Party Games for All Occasions: No More Wallflowers."

One of our teens, who shall remain nameless, often complains, "Why am I supposed to invite that person over if I don't know him?" We always respond, "Uh, duh . . . That's how you get to know him!" A better question might be "*How* am I supposed to invite him over if I don't know him?" It might seem complicated and scary, but it's pretty simple. Just say, "Hey, I'm having a party at my house on Saturday night at seven. Wanna come?" Who doesn't want an invitation to a party? Seriously? Wouldn't you be flattered if someone asked you a simple question like that? Everyone wants to be wanted.

Well, of course, that person has to decide if you're cool enough, but that's his problem. You've extended the hand of friendship. It's his loss if he declines. I guess he's not a gem. Now rinse and repeat.

PARTY TIP

Expect half of the people you want to come over to not be able to make it because of schedule conflicts. Decide how many people you want at your party and then invite about twice that number. Out of those who say they will come, some will flake at the last minute, so then you'll end up with about the right number. Kind of weird, but it's reality.

PARTY DIP

So that your parents don't freak out and have to get a loan to pay for all of your party food, just ask people to bring a snack to share. One of my sons kept a written list of people he invited and what food everyone was bringing so that he could be organized and help me know what I needed to provide to supplement the snackage. Before the party, he would text everyone a reminder, light candles around the house for ambiance, spray potpourri so the house smelled good, and then make sure we had everything out for the activities or games. He rocked the house.

Do you want to know a secret? Your parents probably *hope* that your house becomes the cool hangout for your friends. It's true. Help clean up the house before and after your shindig and your parents will be so impressed that they'll encourage you to throw another one.

Now, don't get me wrong. I'm not saying you're supposed to throw big parties every weekend. Just be brave and try it. Most of the time, you'll just be inviting one or two friends at a time to do something fun. You don't have to create an entire Broadway production to have a good time and create memories. You'll get to know more kids at school and that simply makes being at school better.

Here's one more story about my teen years in school. My twin sister and I have always loved being twins. We used to dress alike for many years until we finally figured out we could have twice the wardrobe if we bought separate outfits. (Hey, I never said we were the sharpest tools in the shed, if you know what I mean.) By the time we got to high school, we would dress alike only on rare occasions. Everyone got a kick out of it and we would really play it up for fun. Except there was this one girl who would mock us and yell, "Oooooh! Look at the little twinsies!" She would laugh and make us feel dumb for celebrating our "twinness." On my more confident days, I could easily blow her off, but there were other days when she really made me feel stupid and insecure. Wait, let me rephrase that: I *allowed* her to make me feel stupid and insecure.

Remember, your attitude is your choice. I had to work hard at not allowing her words to bother me. The truth is that there will always be someone who makes you feel like a loser. They obviously don't know you and your great potential, so just ignore them and move on. Your best comeback line is to completely ignore what was said and walk away.

GOOD COMEBACK LINES FOR BULLIES

- Oh, I get it . . . like humor, but different.
- Feel better now?
- I hear you, but I'm not listening.
- Build up your self-esteem some other way.
- Just words.
- Are you going to waste my time like this every day?
- Dude. That's hilarious.
- Thanks!
- I don't know what your problem is, but I'll bet it's hard to pronounce.
- You remind me of myself when I was like you.
- Wait a minute. I'm trying to imagine you with a kind personality.
- Have a nice day . . . somewhere else.
- Good one!

But wait! There's more to the story and you're going to love this. Many years later I heard that she had gotten married and had given birth to twins! Yes! There *is* justice in this world! The story gets even better. Wait for it . . . she then gave birth to another set of twins! You can't make this stuff up!

Needless to say, I'm sure her attitude has changed about twins and about making fun of people.

By the way, if you're a twin, you *have* to go to the annual Twins Days Festival in Twinsburg, Ohio! It's held the first weekend of every August and is super cheesy but super fun! My twin sister and I went together one year to celebrate our birthday. Guess what? My twin sister married a twin! He has a fraternal twin sister, so all four of us went to the festival and also visited all of the Church history sites in Kirtland, Ohio, while we were in the state. It was awesome!

Finally, if you happen to be one of those truly cool people and you're starting to feel a little cocky about it, just remember, your teenage children will think you're a total dork.

FOR THE GUYS' EYES ONLY

Don't worry so much about being cool. My husband says he wasted way too many years and way too much energy on trying to get the approval from others. Here's a tip: just throw on some dark sunglasses. Instant cool. There, done!

For the Lasses with Glasses

Think long-term. When you feel like a total goober and want to sink into a depressive state that involves devouring an entire pint of ice cream (cough . . . personal . . . cough . . . experience), just remember that Heavenly Father thinks you're awesome. I do too.

RANDOM JOKE ABOUT GLASSES

What do you call a fish with no eyes?
A fsh

SUCCESS TIPS FROM MY WISE FRIENDS WHO ARE ALSO COOL

- Every day is a gift! Smile! Expect good things will happen for you! Pray for guidance, honor your values, and make better everyone and everything you touch! —Jenny Jordan Frogley (I asked her to send advice that was twenty-five words or less and she wrote back, "Twenty-five words or less is tough! This is twenty-seven!" You probably recognize her name from EFY music CDs. She has such a beautiful voice! You can watch her sing the song "Never Be Another" that she wrote for her teenage daughter to remind her that she was beautifully unique at: https://www.youtube.com/watch?v=y9csRVs9P7o)

* There is nothing more important than your personal character, morals, and beliefs, which will be challenged often. —Jason McHood Hansen
* Be authentic, always. —Karen McLennan
* The most important days in your life are the day you were born and the day you find out why. —Mark Twain (Okay, so he and I aren't personal friends because he has been dead for over a century, but I really love that quote! You have a unique purpose in this world. The adventure begins when you try to find out what that is and then do it!)

CHAPTER THREE

Reading Glasses: Education Opens Doors and Your Eyes

Speaking of school . . . What? More school?! I can hear you moaning already. More education opens many doors in both our temporal and spiritual pursuits, and expands our vision. With a good education you will have more options for your future. I promise.

Get an education! You will never regret it. I have met *many* adults who tell me they wish they had chosen that path earlier. It's so much harder, although not impossible, to get a college degree later in life. There will be bills to pay, mouths to feed, and little bodies to clothe later on. But now while you're young and free from many adult responsibilities, you can focus your energies on improving yourself and acquiring marketable skills to offer the world. Plus, it's easier when you're young and your parents help pay for it! (Wink)

Can you relate to this version of the scriptures when Jesus was trying to teach?

> Then Jesus took his disciples up on the mountain and gathered them around Him. And He taught them, saying, "Blessed are the poor in spirit . . . Blessed are the meek . . . Blessed are the merciful."
>
> And Simon Peter said, "Do we have to write this stuff down?"
>
> And Philip said, "Will this be on the test?"
>
> And John said, "Sorry, would you mind repeating that?"

> And Andrew said, "John the Baptist's disciples don't have to learn this stuff!"
>
> And Matthew said, "Huh?"
>
> And Judas said, "What does this have to do with real life?"
>
> Then one of the Pharisees, an expert in the law, said, "I don't see any of this in your syllabus. Do you have a lesson plan? Is there a summary? Where is the student guide? Will there be any follow-up assignments? How will this affect the bell curve?"
>
> And Thomas, who had missed the sermon, came to Jesus privately and said, "Did we do anything important yesterday?"

I hope that doesn't sound like you when you're at school or doing homework! I teach culinary students at the world-famous Le Cordon Bleu School and I'm always amazed when they try to sneak out early—as if I won't notice. I remind them that they're paying about $120 a day to *be there*, so if they skip class or leave early, they're simply not getting their money's worth! The point of going to school is to gain knowledge! If we're going to be like God, then we might need to know what an electron is. Do you think that information is going to suddenly appear in your brain without having to learn it?

I remember sitting in a physics class in college, not understanding the lecture and practically falling asleep with boredom. (Hey, I'm human!) Then the professor said, "Now, this was probably the law of nature that Moroni used to bust through Joseph Smith's roof that night." Wait . . . what? Suddenly, I was interested! There's a law of physics for that? (The beautiful thing about BYU is you get to talk about gospel stuff like that right in the middle of any class!)

Now, some people accumulate many degrees and then think they're smarter than God. What an education should do is help us learn to recognize truth. Sadly, not everything your teachers at school tell you is true. (Except for your seminary teachers! All that stuff *is* true!) One of the most

important skills you can develop in school is *how* to learn and how to find the truth in what is being taught.

Another reason to advance your education is to learn what you're passionate about and how you can use your talents to bless the world.

Answer the following questions to help you figure out some possible career paths:

What do you like to do now?

How could you earn money doing that?

What would you like to study in college?

What would you like to be an expert in?

If you think high school is fun, just wait until college! At a university you can learn about life and who you are. College can really open your eyes and teach you how to think "outside the box." What's inside those gigantic textbooks is really great stuff, but even better than that is what you learn about what's inside yourself. For many, going away to college is the first time they're on their own, away from home and parental controls. The good news: you won't have mom around to do your laundry and nag at you to study. The bad news: you won't have mom around to do your laundry and nag at you to study!

Some college kids never learn how to manage their time and budgets, and either flunk out or get kicked out of college. Now is the time to develop self-control so that when you are given more responsibility and freedom in college you will know how to succeed. Next time your dad gets on your back about picking up after yourself, you'll know he's trying to help you develop skills to take care of yourself in the future so your college roommates won't throw you out your dorm window.

Now, I know that after all this talk about *more* school, some of you are rolling your eyes since you're just in the thick of trying to survive your chemistry exams in high school and can't imagine putting up with more annoying teachers or exams that make your head hurt. You're thinking about all of the rich people who hit it big with some invention or multi-marketing scheme without going to college. Good for them. They are the exception, not the rule. If you have some unusual talent and are lucky enough to be in the right place at the right time, you just might hit it big too. I hope you do! But it's probably not a good plan to sit around hoping that will happen.

Even celebrities who are rich and famous appreciate the value of a college degree. Check out the degrees these stars earned:

- Adam Sandler—master's in fine arts from New York University
- Arnold Schwarzenegger—bachelor's in business and International Economics from University of Wisconsin
- Brooke Shields—bachelor's in French literature from Princeton University
- Carrie Underwood—bachelor's in mass communications from Northeastern State University
- Conan O'Brien—bachelor's in American history and literature from Harvard University
- David Spade—bachelor's in business from Arizona State University
- Denzel Washington—bachelor's in theater from Fordham University
- Dwayne "The Rock" Johnson—bachelor's in general studies from University of Miami
- Eva Longoria—bachelor's in kinesiology from Texas A&M University
- J.K. Rowling—bachelor's in French and classical studies from Exeter University
- John Legend—bachelor's in English from the University of Pennsylvania
- Ludacris—bachelor's in music management from Georgia State University
- Matthew McConaughey—bachelor's in film direction from University of Texas at Austin
- Michael Jordan—bachelor's in geography from University of North Carolina
- Natalie Portman—bachelor's in psychology from Harvard University
- Tina Fey—bachelor's in drama from University of Virginia
- Will Ferrell—bachelor's in sports broadcasting from University of Southern California

While you fantasize about being discovered on some reality TV show or getting recruited by an NBA scout when you're shooting hoops in your driveway, be smart and plan for a higher education. Even celebrities with

large bank accounts and only a high school diploma will tell you they would feel proud of themselves if they had gone on to college or some technical school. They know they have missed out on the whole college experience.

Start saving today for college. Try to excel in something now so that you can get that scholarship. If you don't plan for it to happen, it probably won't. Decide now to make it part of your future! Use short-term goals as stepping-stones to long-term goals. Do your homework tonight so you can do well on your test tomorrow. Keep your **EYES** on your goal!

It's not just about learning "stuff." It's about becoming. Doctrine and Covenants 93:36 says, "The glory of God is intelligence." More important than just that college degree hanging on your wall is the knowledge and wisdom you will gain. Part of going to school is simply learning how to learn. Even better is learning to love learning! The mind is like a parachute: it functions only when open. Fill your mind with learning. There is so much cool stuff out there to learn about! For example, no one has yet figured out how cats meow. You should start working on that.

Doctrine and Covenants 90:15 states, "And set in order the churches, and study and learn, and become acquainted with all good books, and with languages, tongues, and people."

Can't stand the thought of sitting in a classroom for one minute longer than you absolutely have to? No worries! If you'd rather sit on your couch with your laptop and take classes online, tons of universities and colleges now offer online degree programs!

Worried that you just don't have the grades for it? No worries! Check out BYU–Idaho's fantastic Pathway program at www.pathway.lds.org. It helps students who want to go to college get on the right path. Get it? "Pathway." I teach BYU–I students from all over the world who are also learning English while they brush up on their skills in math and other subjects. Some of them have just graduated from high school in their country while others are finally achieving their lifetime dream of a college degree after they have raised their children. They sacrifice much to be able to attend BYU–Idaho online. Read this sweet letter from an older student in Mexico who worked really hard in a math class I recently taught online:

Dear Sister Boice,

Hi, How are you? This is our last week. I am really enjoying algebra. I like algebra, but I studied it since 1978. I strive to make each of the exercises. When I do not understand some exercise, and after much effort came to understand it, I feel a great joy!!!! The past week I had a sacred experience. I always ask Heavenly Father, for help before starting to do my homework. Last week was very difficult for me, and when I saw the difficult algebra assignments, I was very nervous.

I asked my Heavenly Father to help me understand in a quick and effective way.

Now I have a stronger testimony of the prayer. He hear me my prayer, I understood algebra, I did my algebra assignments, and I had 100 on the difficult test. I am very grateful to God. I am very grateful with you, for your love, for your comprehension, for your patience, for learn me. Thanks for give me a little more time to deliver my assignments. Thanks for encouraging me to continue . . .

I love you so much.

Ofelia

Isn't that sweet? Do you realize what a privilege it is to go to school? No matter where you are in life, it's a privilege to continue progressing.

Another one of my BYU–I students was from Russia and is currently a famous professional concert pianist there. His name is Gornostaev Vladislove. We called him Vlad. I asked him to share his success tips with you, and the following is what he sent me. I didn't correct his English because I thought it would be fun for you to "hear" his Russian accent.

Even outstanding talent without hard work will never increase. It can not even stay at same level without real efforts. At the end, we'll die. Family happiness requires hard work. Success in career depends on hard work. Hard work is the principle of happiness. Without understanding of this principle, people can not be really happy. Life success is the result of hard work. I'm sure that the most important step in our life, in order to learn how to work hard, is to learn how to keep the commandments.

He was a great example of a hard-working student in my class. (He got an A.) Check out his website at www.gornostaev.net. To read his Russian website in English, click on the "ENG" on the top center of the page. Click on the video on the top right where he plays the piano blindfolded! He and Ofelia are using their college degrees to be disciple-leaders in their countries.

Can't pay for college? No worries! There are tons of scholarships available at www.fastweb.com as well as many other sites online. There is no other time in your life when companies and organizations will throw money at you! Adults love to invest in students with bright futures! Most scholarships require an application, your high school transcript, and an essay. There is *big* money out there for you if you're disciplined and organized enough to start filling out the applications. Start applying during the second half of your junior year in high school. Take thirty minutes once a week to search for them and complete the required paperwork. Keep copies of your essays as Word documents because you can easily tweak them and reuse them on other scholarship forms.

ANOTHER QUICK TIP

Fill out your college applications early. You have a better chance of getting accepted if you beat the "early decision" deadline. It also places you at the front of the line for housing choices!

More interested in a trade school than college? No worries! (Do you see a pattern here?) The point is to learn more so you can earn more. I teach classes at a cooking school in Las Vegas. It's perfect for students who want a career doing something with their hands rather than sitting at some boring desk. The options for you are endless! Don't let your high school be the end of your learning. The prophets have counseled us to be an "ever learning people."

Sterling W. Sill relates the tale of a young man came to Socrates one time and said, "Mr. Socrates, I have come sixteen hundred miles to talk to you about wisdom and learning." He said, "You are a man of wisdom and learning, and I would like to be a man of wisdom and learning. I would like to have you teach me."

Socrates said, "Follow me," and he led the way down to the seashore. They waded out into the water up to their waists, and then Socrates turned on his new student and held his head under the water. His friend struggled and kicked and bucked and tried to get away, but Socrates held him down. Now if you hold someone's head under the water long enough, he will eventually become fairly peaceable. After this man had stopped struggling, Socrates laid him out on the bank to dry, and he went back to the market place.

After the young man had dried out a little bit and recovered from the shock of almost being drowned, he went back to Socrates to find the reason for this rather unusual behavior. Socrates said to him, "When your head was under the water what was the one thing you wanted more than anything else?" And the man said, "More than anything else, I wanted air." Socrates said, "All right, when you want wisdom and learning like you wanted air, you won't have to ask anybody to give it to you." (*BYU Speeches*, 9 February 1965)

Breathe in deeply, my friends!

FOR THE GUYS' EYES ONLY

It's especially important for you guys, the traditional breadwinners, to choose a career path that is valuable in society. It will be hard to support your family if the only thing you are really good at is playing video games. Choose a career that will allow you to make a contribution to the world and meet the needs of society.

The vocation you choose may affect so many things in your life because of the income it will or won't produce, such as:

- Where you live—will you be able to afford a tiny apartment, or have enough for a luxurious home with your own pool and tennis court?
- What kind of vacations you enjoy—will you only be able to afford to rent a video on Saturday night, or have enough to spend a relaxing week at a beach resort in the Bahamas?
- How much you can help your family—will you have to ask your relatives for money, or will you be a financial blessing to your family?
- What Church callings you can hold—will you be too busy with a second job in order to make ends meet, or will you be a tool the Lord can use to build His kingdom on earth?

Money isn't the most important thing in life, but it touches everything that is.

Don't sit on your pair of glasses and break them. In other words, don't quit school and cut off your future possibilities. If you don't feel like studying now, then you need to get used to the phrase "Would you like fries with that?" because you'll be saying it a lot in your future.

For the Lasses with Glasses

While I was growing up, my father was adamant that my two sisters and I did *nothing* until after we graduated from college, even if it was something good like a mission or marriage. He encouraged us to plan for an unknown future by asking us, "What if you never marry and you have to support yourself financially for the rest of your life? What if your husband dies? What if he divorces you and leaves you with no financial support to care for your children? What if he is the only breadwinner in the family and suddenly becomes disabled and you have to provide the financial strength for the family?"

Of course, my sisters and I never planned on any of those terrible things happening, but we knew they were realistic enough that they certainly could happen, and so we recognized the wisdom in being prepared. Read that sentence again. I wrote it several years ago when I first started putting this book together. How could we have ever known that years later, my oldest sister's husband would die from cancer at an early age, leaving her to raise their children alone? Thankfully, she had taken my father's advice to heart and had even earned a PhD! She has been able to get a job that pays her well and also gives her flexibility to be home when her kids return from school. My other sister's husband was recently laid off from his job, so now she is the sole income-earner in her family with six kids! Thankfully, she also has several degrees and can provide for her family while he looks for another job. I'm so grateful for a father who insisted that his daughters be educated and for a Heavenly Father who wants the same for all of us.

As women, we can't expect to marry a rich man who will take care of our every want and need. As women in the Church, we hope to be mothers in this life and in a financial position where we can stay at home with the children to raise them, but that doesn't always happen. LDS girls need to be smart and prepare themselves financially in case that "Brother Right" scenario never comes along.

President Howard W. Hunter said, "There are impelling reasons for our sisters to plan toward employment also. We want them to obtain all the education and vocational training possible before marriage. If they become widowed or divorced and need to work, we want them to have dignified and rewarding employment. If a sister does not marry, she has every right to engage in a profession that allows her to magnify her talents and gifts" ("Prepare for Honorable Employment," *Ensign*, Nov. 1975, 122).

President Hinckley counseled the young women,

> Find purpose in your life. Choose the things you would like to do, and educate yourselves to be effective in their pursuit. . . . Study your options. Pray to the Lord earnestly for direction. Then pursue your course with resolution. The whole gamut of human endeavor is now open to women. There is not anything that you cannot do if you will set your mind to it. You can include in the dream of the woman you would like to be a picture of one qualified to serve society and make a significant contribution to the world of which she will be a part. ("How Can I Become the Woman of Whom I Dream?" *Ensign*, May 2001)

An education isn't just for a career in the business world. George Q. Cannon admonished the young women of the Church when he said, "Too great care cannot be taken in educating our young ladies. To their hands will be mainly committed the formation of the moral and intellectual character of the young. Let the women of our country be made intelligent, and their children will certainly be the same. The proper education of a man decides his welfare, but the interests of a whole family are secured by the correct education of a woman" (Gospel Truth, sel. Jerreld L. Newquist, 1974, 2:138).

How blessed your children will be if you can be the kind of mother who can introduce them to the world of art, literature, science, or music! A good education teaches you many things you don't know, but it extends further than that; it teaches you things you don't even know you don't know!

A safe, good public school education may not be an option to your children in your future world. If you had to home school your children, what kind of an education would they get from you? Would you be able to answer all of their questions or know where to go to find the answers? Would you be able to instill in them a love for learning?

RANDOM JOKE ABOUT GLASSES

"Wow," said Jill after she saw that her friend got glasses.

"You like my new glasses?" asked Scott.

"Yep. They make you look really smart," replied Jill.

"I know. That's what my mom said. That's why I wear them in math class."

SUCCESS TIPS FROM MY WISE FRIENDS WHO WEAR SMARTY PANTS

- There will always be someone better than you, but you can decide if there will ever be someone who works harder. —Peter Hollens (I've been following his awesome YouTube channel for over a year now and adore him and his talents. When I asked him to send me some words of advice for you, he said, "My son just came to the world, and I really needed to spend the first week with him as much as possible. Isn't that amazing??? Not many people get to say that, ha." Go listen to his music right now on his YouTube channel!)
- Have the confidence that you can learn anything, and the humility to admit that you don't know everything. —J. Andrews
- Internalize the principle of serving others as early as possible in life. A person finds happiness by serving unmet needs. But a selfish, inward focus brings insecurities and lack of fulfillment. Follow Aristotle's advice that rings true still today: "Where the needs of the world and your talents cross, therein lies your vocation." —Tom Tam
- Don't rely on school lessons for all of your learning. The best thinkers in education—Dewey, Montessori, Vygotsky—all believed we learn more from the things we do in the real world, and the people we meet and talk with, rather than just textbooks. Lead your own learning process. —Ryan Rose Weaver (She helped create the innovative Big World Network online where people can read books in episodes, like on TV! She's also a fantastic author. Check out www.BigWorldNetwork.com.)

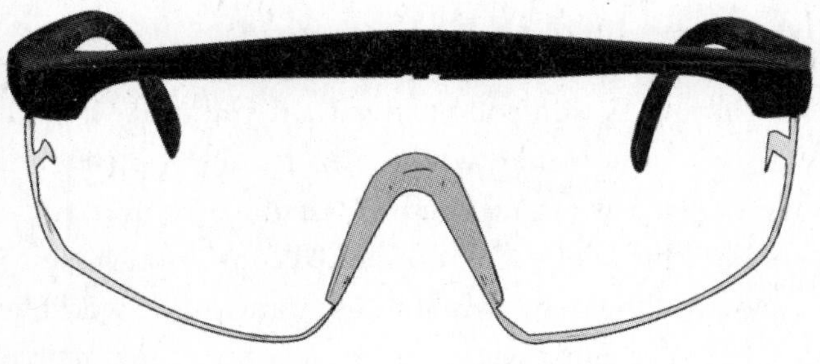

CHAPTER FOUR

Science Safety Goggles: Dating Is a Science

Here's an easy science experiment: if a glass is filled halfway with water, is it half empty or half full? I'll bet you've heard that one before. The surprise is that there is no wrong answer—it's a choice. It's all a matter of how you **LOOK** at it. Most people start the day in neutral, reacting to whatever happens to them during the day. The surprising truth is that you can *create* your day.

Imagine creating your own world. As members of the Church, we often talk about how some day we'll earn entrance into the celestial kingdom where we will be gods and goddesses and can create our own worlds. We imagine creating beautiful snow-capped mountains that we can ski down, and then, because it's our world, we can ski back up! I'm sure there's some kind of scientific formula for that, right?

So, what does science have to do with dating? Well, it's a scientifically proven formula that shows you marry whom you date. (Be impressed that I correctly used the word "whom.") The selection process begins when you decide whether to date someone. You'll never marry him or her unless you date first. Duh. So *now* is the time to make the decision of who it will be! No, I don't mean the actual person, but rather the type of person. Double duh.

Now is the time to make the decision about the kind of person you want to spend the rest of your life with while your head is clear. When you're in love, your heart and your hormones can easily take over your brain. It's a fact. You can make certain decisions right now, and later you can fill in more details as you gain experience with different kinds of personalities and

choices. You're in the "gathering information" stage right now.

Don't get fixated on one kind of person or even hair color. Date jocks *and* nerds, blondes *and* brunettes. Just like when you go shopping for shoes, try on lots of different styles. You might even be surprised at which one fits better than you had originally thought.

When I was your age, I had two lists of qualities to help me determine the guy I wanted to marry:

- *Has* to be . . .

* Would be nice to be . . .

The items on my first list were non-negotiable. The second list had things I was looking for in a guy, but if he didn't have them, they weren't deal breakers. For example, these are some of the things I had on my lists to help me narrow down my search for the perfect husband:

* **Has to be:** person of integrity, kind, returned missionary, college graduate, temple worthy, funny, smart, tall, handsome, hard worker, family man, loves to travel, will be a good dad, responsible, dependable.
* **Would be nice to be:** plays the guitar, speaks Spanish with me, can ballroom dance with me, has a strong brotherhood with friends we can share our life with, knows how to build things, can fix anything, good genes, good jeans, has computer hacking skills (just kidding on that last one).

Notice, I forgot to include "filthy, stinkin' rich" on either list. Dang it! What was I thinking? What's on your list?

Write it here.

1. Has to be:

2. Would be nice to be:

When I was in college, I was completely in love with this one guy and could seriously see myself marrying him. He even had *all* the qualities on my "would be nice to have" list! He was perfect! After dating for many months, I finally started noticing some red flags that made me realize he was missing one very important quality: integrity. No biggie, right? Wrong.

I simply didn't feel like I could trust the guy. How are you supposed to trust your life *and* your eternity into the hands of someone who isn't completely honest? Someone with a lack of integrity has the potential to have an affair after you're married. I really worried about that because my parents had divorced due to infidelity. Someone who is dishonest in business could cause my future family to fall into financial ruin. Someone who isn't true to the Lord could become less active or even leave the Church. I realized that missing that one simple quality was a deal breaker for me. Integrity suddenly jumped to the very top of my list of "has to be."

Another quality that seemed to be of utmost importance to a successful marriage was kindness. I had watched married couples bicker and fight over the dumbest things and thought it looked so ugly. I remember going to a family's house for dinner and hearing the parents snap at each other over trivial matters all night long in front of us. Awkward. I was shocked they would act so childishly in front of us and everyone felt uncomfortable just being in their house with them. Marry someone who is kind. Life is rough and you simply don't want to spend it with someone who nitpicks over every one of your imperfections. Yeah, I said it. You have imperfections. We all do. Deal with it.

You've heard of a "nagging wife," right? Girls, don't be one of those. Constantly complaining and whining about every little thing will cause your husband to fall out of love faster than almost anything else. Gaining six hundred pounds is the other romance killer for guys. Girls, don't do that either.

Guys, you're not off the hook here. Be *very* careful what you say to girls. Your words can haunt her for years. You have no idea. Those seemingly

innocent words can come back to bite you. Be afraid. Be very afraid.

While you're busy making your lists and looking for that perfect person, remember that you should be developing those qualities yourself, because they're probably on your future spouse's list too!

Make these decisions right now and commit to keeping your commitments.

Write down what you will and will not accept:

My future spouse will be

My future spouse would never

My future spouse always

My future spouse has

My future spouse does

My future spouse can't

My future spouse is

Here we are talking about marriage and we haven't even discussed dating yet! If you're sixteen, go for it! (The dating part, not marriage yet!) Go on lots of group dates and you'll avoid some of the awkward and dangerous one-on-one moments. If you're younger, please recognize the wisdom in waiting until you're a couple of years older. You can still go to youth dances and have a blast.

When I was in high school, all of the girls felt pressure to have a boyfriend. The "good" boyfriends were even expected to buy a diamond ring for their girls! That's ridiculous! I had some great boyfriends, and one even bought me a diamond ring. But years later, I wish that I had actually spent more time getting to know the girls rather than being so focused on only a few boys. You can keep friends of your same gender your whole lifetime, but it's inappropriate to keep in touch with old flames when you're married to someone else. You feel me?

Pairing off with a boyfriend or girlfriend before a mission is simply dangerous. Hormones are raging and you develop deep attachments that make leaving each other for eighteen months or two years painful. I know everyone at your school is probably pairing off, but they probably haven't heard the prophet's counsel not to—*you* have. I'm thinking that the prophet is probably wiser than your friends.

You need to date a lot of different kinds of people before you can intelligently make the best choice for a marriage partner. Because we get married in temples, you're going to be stuck with . . . I mean, be sealed to this person for time *and* all eternity, so you better pick carefully!

Here I am talking about marriage again. Let's get back to the basics on dating. Like, how do you start a conversation anyway? It's easy: just open your mouth. Seriously, it's not as hard as it seems. Walk up to someone cute and ask:

- Hey, I think I'm lost. Do you know where ______is?
- I've never seen you at school before. Are you new here?
- Did you see that guy with the green Mohawk today?
- That's a cool backpack. Do you think it would fit my skateboard in there?

Here's the trick: ask questions. People are flattered when they think someone is genuinely interested in them. Here are some more examples:

- So what did you think of that school rally today?
- My sister would love that jacket you're wearing. Where did you buy it?
- I'm doing a survey for a project. How do you feel about YouTube videos with cats in them?

Don't ask yes or no questions, but ask open-ended ones that get the other person thinking and talking. Here are even more examples:

- I noticed you were reading that book. What is it about?
- I noticed your cool cell phone. I'm thinking about switching. What features do you like about it?
- I'm doing a survey about popular mobile apps. Which ones do you like the best?

Who says you're *not* doing a survey? It's the truth, after all, if you're asking a bunch of people the same question, right? It doesn't have to be published on a website or some place to be legit. Am I right or am I right?

Everyone likes to laugh, so if you can start out a conversation with something funny, even better. The first time my husband called me on the phone (after we had met in person) he asked, "So, do you know how to get a pot pie out of the cardboard holder without breaking it?" It made me laugh, as well as make me feel like I was rescuing a helpless bachelor.

I always tell my sons to boldly go up to the most gorgeous girl on campus and say, "My mom wants me to date someone beautiful so that she has good-looking grandchildren." For some reason, they just can't bring themselves to say that.

Here are a few LDS pick-up lines that might work if you are brave and funny enough to pull it off:

- The 13th Article of Faith requires me to ask you out. ("If there is anything virtuous, lovely or of good report, or praiseworthy, we seek after these things.")
- Even with the Liahona, I get lost in your eyes.
- You remind me of the fruit in Lehi's dream: precious above all others.
- Can I introduce you to my friends to prove that angels really do exist?
- I want to be like the Spirit, to be with thee whithersoever thou goest.
- What's your favorite temple? I'm looking at mine.
- I would leave ninety-nine sheep to come find you. Then I would carry you home joyfully on my shoulder.
- I just got back from my mission and I'm looking for my next companion!
- Are you the iron rod? Because I want to hold onto you for the rest of eternity.
- Is your name Virtue? Because you garnish my thoughts unceasingly.
- Are you a Gadianton robber? Because you just stole my heart.
- Are you the sword of Laban? Because your workmanship is exceedingly fine!

Okay, well, at least you'll make her laugh. That's a *great* start! Of course, if she's not LDS, she won't understand any of those and she'll be laughing *at* you instead of *with* you.

A friend and I created a dating app that features fun things to do in Rexburg, Idaho. If you're a BYU–Idaho student, you'll love it! It's called

"DatingU." My free app for BYU in Provo will be coming out soon. Get creative on your dates. The point is to get to know the other person, so just sitting in a dark theater won't tell you much.

FOR THE GUYS' EYES ONLY

What are girls attracted to?

- Personality—someone who makes them laugh and is kind.
- Looks—there has to be chemistry.
- Drive—they want a guy who has goals.
- Talent—they want you to be their hero.

My third son was pretty shy, but he knew he wanted to develop better social skills. He and his buddies would gather at our house for a big pep talk on the weekends and then they'd head out to a mall or other teen hangout in town to play "Go!" The rules were that if someone in the group spotted a cute girl, he would point to one of the guys and say, "Go!" If the guy chickened out, he'd have to do twenty pushups right then and there. Which was worse: trying to talk to a girl or doing pushups in public? At first, it was really awkward and hard for all of them, but by the end of the night they would all return to our house with stories of victory and even a few phone numbers. Of course, they were too chicken to *use* the phone numbers, but now they knew they could get them!

The point is: just be brave. Open your mouth and ask her out. The worst thing that could happen is she'll laugh at you and say no. You can survive that. She's only laughing and turning you down because she doesn't know how awesome you are. That's okay. There are about a billion other girls out there, so ask someone else. Just do it. You can do it.

Until you can fly solo, get a good wingman, someone who can walk up to a cute girl and make you sound awesome. My son who played "Go!" had all kinds of secret hand signals with his buddies. The signals were to let them know when he needed backup to keep a conversation going with a cute girl or to come rescue him when it was going terribly wrong.

Here's something you need to know: girls run in packs. You've probably already discovered that. For example, when you go out to dinner or to a dance with other couples, suddenly all the girls have to go to the restroom together. Yes, they're capable of going by themselves, but they rarely do. Why? Women's restrooms aren't just for "business"; they're where the girls can talk freely about you guys and how your date is going. It's where they can get feedback from their friends.

Here's the thing: girls *have* to talk. In an average day, women use 143,783 words. Men have already used up their allotted 12,432 by the end of work or school. Okay, that may be a bit exaggerated, but not by much. Talking about everything is how women process information and emotions.

Here's another tip: be a gentleman and the girls will swoon. Yeah, they might want to date a "bad boy," but they want to marry the knight in shining armor. This goes against what I said about dating the kind of person you want to marry, but they're still figuring that out. Be patient with them. Be a gentleman and open doors for girls. Of course girls are capable of opening their own doors. Some feminist girls are so insistent about proving to the world that they're equal to men that they forget to be women. If you find yourself with one of these stubborn women, then just keep opening the door for her. (Or pick a different girl.) She may resist at first, but deep down she is glowing inside that she has found such a gentleman. She probably didn't know they really exist. She wants to feel special and important to you. Insist on being a gentleman and soon that soft woman inside will emerge and she'll feel more comfortable being feminine, not feminist.

Want to score even bigger points? After you open her car door and she slides on to her seat, reach over and hand her the seat belt. She'll be totally impressed.

Do you want to know another secret? You can get any girl you want. Even the most beautiful girl in the world has insecurities and will be flattered by your attention (unless she's a spoiled egomaniac with no manners). Don't let a talented, gorgeous, smart girl psyche you out. Just go for it.

For the Lasses with Glasses

What are guys attracted to?

- Looks—they'll do anything for your beauty.
- Personality—they want someone who is easy to get along with and fun to be around.
- Admiration—they want someone who makes them feel like a hero.

It is *super* nerve-wracking for a guy to talk to you. You have no idea how much courage it takes for him to start a conversation with you. You're pretty and scary. Make it easier for him. Be kind. If you're not interested, let him down gently. He'll feel defeated, so you could always say something like, "No, I can't go out with you, but I know a girl who thinks you're really cute!" Of course, don't say that unless you can quickly think of someone else.

If a guy asks to marry you, before answering him be sure to ask *where*. There is no substitute for the temple. A new member of a bishopric was speaking to the youth in his ward at a fireside with his lovely wife at his side. He said, "She deserves much of the credit for my present course in life. When we were dating years ago, I took her for a ride in my car to a secluded area. We parked. As I started to make some intimate advances that she felt were improper, she said, 'All of my life I have planned on being married in the temple. Don't you disqualify me!'" She had charted her course before she got into troubled waters.

By the way, there is nothing wrong with you if you aren't dating. Society makes us feel like we should be going out every weekend or else we're complete losers. This whole process takes time, so don't be so impatient. Maybe you're a late bloomer. There's nothing wrong with that. Maybe the guys around you are too shy, especially if they're young and haven't served a mission yet. When they return home from their missions, they'll know how to knock on your door and be courageous enough to talk to you.

Until then, nurture your relationships with friends. Romance will come along soon enough. I know that sometimes you feel lonely and you just want that special someone to be with you already. It's hard to wait. He is out there thinking about you too. Do you have all of the qualities he is expecting you to have already? Are you his dream girl yet? If not, you've got some work to do on yourself to be ready for him. It takes time. If you do it right, you'll be with that special person *forever*! Surely, you can wait another minute before you meet him. Do it right.

Did you feel that just now? That's me giving you a virtual hug.

RANDOM JOKE ABOUT GLASSES

Soon after their last child left home for college, an older husband and wife were sitting on the couch with a newspaper. The wife took off the man's reading glasses so they could talk. She lovingly said, "You know, honey, without your glasses on you look like the same handsome young man I married thirty years ago." "Sweetheart," he replied, "without my glasses on, you still look pretty good too!"

SUCCESS TIPS FROM MY WISE FRIENDS WHO KNOW A THING OR TWO ABOUT TRUE LOVE

- I've always been inspired by the American writer Oscar Wilde who said, "Be yourself because everyone else is taken." Just be your best self. —Susan Horrocks Plessinger
- Learn to give sincere compliments and practice giving them often. —Richard Maycock
- Surround yourself with people who value, appreciate, respect, and honor your essence to the best of their ability. You will learn to realize who is your friend and who is not by observing who respects your boundaries and who doesn't. Everyone makes mistakes. Those who admit, apologize, and grow above ignorance are the friends worth keeping around. —Nick Giordano (He's a super sweet guy who goes to the same martial arts dojo as my sons. He's a spiritual artist who uses interesting symbolism in his artwork. Check out his cool T-shirt designs at https://www.facebook.com/WonLoveInc.)
- Always be kinder than is necessary. —Catherine Reese Newton
- Treat others how you would like to be treated and always tell the truth. —Brenda Brockly Boissevain

CHAPTER FIVE

How Much Is That Mormon in the Window?

Money. Money. Money. You need it now and you're going to need it in the future. Let's dispel the old myth that money is evil. In all fairness, it's the *love* of money that is evil not money itself. It's the importance you place on that piece of paper that matters not how much of it you have or don't have. Money is important in this world of ours. Life is expensive. You're going to need to know how to get some.

When I turned sixteen years old I got my first "real" job. I rode my bike (uphill both ways, of course) to my job at a French pastry shop (*mmm*). When I got my first paycheck I couldn't believe how rich I was, and I went out and bought presents for all of my family. Although my parents were pleased with my enthusiastic generosity, they wanted me to save my money for the future. There's that word again: future. How fun is that? Those paychecks seemed to accumulate quickly, but now that I'm grown up, my money hardly has time to be saved before I'm using it to pay bills. Boo!

Do you have any idea how much money your parents spend on just "life"? Right off the top, they pay ten percent of their income in tithing! Then Uncle Sam swipes a bunch more off the top. What's left is used to pay for housing to put a roof over your head, medical insurance, auto insurance, a car loan or other transportation, gas, groceries, utilities (air conditioning is worth every penny), auto repairs, home maintenance, education, your field trips, your allowance, clothing for the entire family, pet care, vacations, charity, missionary fund, trips to the doctor, entertainment, emergencies, gifts to others, and your lunch money! Can you see why they might be annoyed when you ask them for more money?

QUICK EXPERIMENT

Go ask your mom or dad for money right now. Go on, do it. Then, come back and tell me what they said. Well, what was their response? Yeah, I thought so.

In order to get some of that green paper, you're going to need a *marketable* skill, one that will actually earn money when used. A degree in ancient Chinese basketry, although fascinating to some, is not in high demand and will probably get you a job that doesn't even pay enough to buy diapers for Junior. Yes, some day you may actually be the adult buying the diapers in your family. Hard to believe, I know. On the other hand, learning Chinese in today's global economy is a terrific idea and an increasingly useful skill to have!

Choose an education that will give you specific skills that will help make you marketable. You may have to read this twice: *the amount of money you receive will always be in direct ratio to the demand for what you do, your ability to do it, and the difficulty of replacing you.* Get it? Got it? Good.

Teenagers can't wait to grow up and be on their own. Being an adult looks so great, right? So, where are you going to get the money to pay for all the stuff you think is so awesome? In an earlier chapter we talked about getting more education past high school because that will help you to earn more money. That's a start.

Experience also helps. How do you get experience if you're only thirteen or looking for your first job? Ah, that's the old "Catch 22"—you can't get hired unless you have experience and you can't get experience unless you're hired! Frustrating, I know, but you *can* get experience without necessarily even getting paid at a job. How about all of those service hours you spent in Scouts or on your Young Women's value projects? What about all the hours you spent helping your dad with his construction business? That could go on your resume to show a potential boss that you've developed certain skills. Even babysitting shows a certain amount of responsibility and work ethic.

QUICK DEFINITION

"Catch 22" is an expression that was first used in a novel written in 1961 by Joseph Heller. He used it as a military regulation in his book, but it means when you're trapped in a situation by contradictory conditions.

My oldest son was fortunate to get his first job at age fifteen because the owner of a local movie theater was a member of our ward. My son worked hard, accepted all of the crummy tasks, and by the time he was sixteen, he already had a strong employer reference to put on his resume for future jobs. One of his friends also wanted a job there, but the owner wasn't hiring anyone else at the time. Timing can be everything.

One day a super popular movie was being released and the movie theater had a big carnival to attract more customers. Now you're going to think I'm making this up when you read this next part. My son's friend just showed up and volunteered to help out at the carnival for free. He helped clean up, passed out free samples of ice cream, greeted guests, and was so willing to do anything that they ended up hiring him at the end of the day! They were so impressed by his eagerness to work and positive attitude that they knew they wanted an employee like that and would make room for him in their company. He got the job while other kids wanting to work there just dropped off their applications and waited to hear back from the manager. *Go out there and get what you want!*

By the way, if you're an entrepreneur at heart, you should definitely be watching shows on TV like "Shark Tank." Contact the companies you see featured on that show and find out what they did to be successful. If you want to be successful, do what successful people do.

Another point I want to make with that example is to be willing to take the jobs that might be considered yucky. You will be recognized for your team spirit and eventually get the better jobs. If you can prove yourself valuable with small things, you will be rewarded with big things soon enough!

TOP TEN WORST JOBS EVER

- Portable toilet cleaner
- Cat food quality controller
- Roadkill remover
- Chris Brown's publicist

- ✳ DMV employee
- ✳ Taser tester
- ✳ Embalmer
- ✳ Telemarketer
- ✳ Medical waste biohazard cooker
- ✳ Shark suit tester

When I was in college I worked in Washington, DC, as an intern for a congressman. I had great hopes of changing the world and thought of myself as the girl version of *Mr. Smith Goes to Washington* (great movie you need to see some time!), and I was so proud to serve my country. I really wanted to make a difference and prove that I was a deep thinking, valuable contributor to our country. I was assigned to work on several projects and thought I was doing a pretty good job, but I wasn't getting a lot of attention from the congressman . . . yet.

Each week a different intern was chosen as "Intern of the Week." I had no idea what that meant, but the title sounded very impressive and it was an accolade I strived for. Then the long-awaited day I arrived. I was told that I had been chosen as the "Intern of the Week." I was thrilled! My assignment was to arrive an hour early, open up the office, prepare the congressman's office, go through the mail that had gathered overnight, and get the rest of the office ready for the day. I was so excited that I arrived two hours early! I just knew that this would be my week to shine! After I had finished the assigned tasks, I still had a half hour before anyone would even be arriving in the office.

I noticed the office bathroom and kitchenette were pretty disgusting because no one in the office ever had time to clean it, so I decided to straighten things up and do some extra cleaning. When the congressman arrived and saw what I had done, he was completely amazed. He couldn't stop talking about how great the bathroom looked. You would have thought I had cured cancer or balanced the national budget by how much he praised me. All this time I had been trying to impress him with my clever mind and political acumen only to finally catch his attention by being willing to clean the doggone toilet!

It taught me a great lesson. No small deed goes unnoticed. You might think some jobs or tasks are beneath you. But when you are willing to do them, you show humility, a willingness to learn, and a good work ethic that will impress even the toughest critic. I know a teenager (one of my . . .cough . . .sons) who never wanted a menial job because he said that it's not what he sees himself doing in the future. He refused to work at a fast-food restaurant or at the grocery store or take any entry-level job. Guess what? He never got a job. He now has no work experience and is embarrassed by his résumé, as he is getting close to graduating from college. Another teen (his wiser brother who started working at fifteen at the movie theater) is also graduating from college and has quite an impressive résumé that proves he is a hard worker. Who do you think is going to get hired first?

Speaking of references, ask people who have seen you work hard in various situations to write a letter of recommendation for you that you can present to future employees. Oftentimes a good letter or two will get your foot in the door, especially if you've never had a "real job" before. Ask your seminary teacher, Young Men's or Young Women's leader, bishop, or even your home teacher to write the letter of recommendation. Make copies and include them when you fill out a job application. You can even use them when you're applying for college scholarships later on.

How do you write a résumé if you don't have very much work experience? There are a million websites online that will teach you how to write a résumé. The trick is to feature your talents and abilities rather than your work experience when you don't have any.

Almost all of you will spend forty years in the work force. If you work forty hours a week, you'll work two thousand hours per year and eighty thousand hours in a lifetime. That's a long time to work at something you don't enjoy! It's better to work at a yucky job now and get experience for a better job than to be stuck at a job you don't enjoy for life. The objective in choosing a career is to discover one's genius. By genius I mean those things that you do with excellence and that you enjoy doing. What is your passion? What do you do that makes you get excited? What could you make a YouTube channel about?

Write down the things you would be willing to do for a living:

☀

☀

☀

What if you didn't get paid very much money to do them? Would you still be willing to do them?

Now, write down what you are passionate about and would do for a living, even if you didn't get paid very much to do them:

☀

*

*

Finally, who would be willing to pay you to do it?

*

*

*

Whether you earn a little bit of money or a lot, you need to learn how to manage your money, before it manages you. Here's the secret to being rich:

* Earn more money.
* Spend less money.

Pick one or do both! But remember that simply earning more money doesn't make you richer; you have to know what to do with it. Become a wise consumer shopper. There are tons of websites where you can get cost comparisons on various products and companies. Shop around for the best deal. The prophets continuously counsel us to stay out of debt. Don't spend more than you have! Benjamin Franklin gave us the secret to wealth. He said that the road to wealth lies in augmenting our means or diminishing our wants. That's a fancy way of saying, "Earn more or spend less." Either will do, but the quickest way to wealth is to do both at the same time. The Church teaches us to rely on ourselves and to not expect a handout from the government, other people, or the bishop.

Get comfortable using coupons and saving money now so that it's not so painful later. Right now you probably don't have the pressure of paying all the bills in your family, right? Start demonstrating discipline now. Many adults get into serious debt problems or drown under credit card misuse because they never learned how to use their money wisely.

You're already old enough to have a savings account at a bank and maybe even a checking account. Some banks and credit unions will give children and teens incentives for opening an account or for every time you deposit money into your account. Take advantage of those special deals. Most of the time the reward is cold, hard cash! Boom!

Credit cards can be extremely dangerous to people with no self-control. But if you can discipline your spending habits, they can help establish good credit. You generally have to be eighteen years old to get a credit card account. Every time you open an account with a credit card company or even get one of those store credit cards, your every purchase and payment will be recorded by another company whose sole existence is to track your habits and determine if you are trustworthy with your financial obligations.

Actually, there are three national companies that track your usage. Later in life when you get ready to make a large purchase such as a house or car or even to rent an apartment, your credit record will be looked at. Did you know that? Missing a credit card payment or rent payment even one month will show up as a big red flag. If your record shows you are irresponsible, you may not be able to get a school loan from a bank, get a mortgage to buy a house, or even buy that cool car you really want. You might not even be allowed to rent a car!

Now is the time to start proving you can control your spending. Be responsible and make your payments on time every month. You'll find that as soon as you can prove to one credit card company that you're good with money, then every credit card company around will want to offer you their card. Be careful. *Always* pay off your card in full every month! Did you hear me? *Always*! Only make a purchase with your credit card if you know you have that much money in your bank account today. The Lord has counseled us to get out of debt. That includes credit card debt. A better plan of action is to simply not get into debt! Ever!

By the way, I wrote a book about saving and earning money. It has tons of ideas and helpful apps you'll love. It's often offered for free on Amazon's Kindle, so grab it when it becomes available. Free is my jam! It's called *How to Stay UP in a DOWN Economy.*

To put all of this money talk into perspective, remember that in all your seeking, "seek ye first the kingdom of God." *If you don't, it will not matter in the end what you have put first instead.* While you're busy earning the big bucks, remember to pay your tithing first. The Lord has promised you blessings if you will be obedient to this principle. Trust Him. Make it a habit to pay fast offerings as well. Jesus told of a widow who gave a small amount of money when compared to others who were quite wealthy and gave little. Whatever amount you offer each month will bless at least two people: you and the person who will receive it!

Money is simply an earthly concept that we can use to acquire heavenly qualities. How we use our money shows Heavenly Father where our priorities are. Is money more important to us than spending time with our families or keeping the Sabbath day holy? Do we use our money to help other people and as a tool to bless others? Money is simply a tool to help us achieve things that are long lasting, like education or building family relationships or strengthening the kingdom of God. Avoiding the love of money will come when we use our "riches . . . to do good" (Jacob 2:19).

Money
Prem Rawat

It can buy a house, but not a home.
It can buy a bed, but not sleep.
It can buy a clock, but not time.
It can buy you a book, but not knowledge.
It can buy you a position, but not respect.
It can buy you medicine, but not health.
It can buy you blood, but not life.
It can buy you sex, but not love.

I mentioned earlier that I teach several different classes online for BYU–Idaho. I'm always humbled when I teach the math class for international students. One of the big projects in the class is to create a budget. Many of them have never done that before. As they submit their work, I am able to see what they're spending money on. Most of the European students have to carefully budget for gas because it is so expensive there. Many of the African students are so poor they have to decide whether to spend their extra money on shoes or food for their families. Can you imagine?

And you want to know why your parents get annoyed when you want to spend $150 on athletic shoes. We call that "First World Problems."

Whenever I speak to audiences about money, I like to do this object lesson that helps put money into its proper perspective. I ask the audience to raise their hands if they consider themselves to be world-class rich. Most everyone in the room laughs and curiously looks around to see if anyone is actually that rich (and how quickly they should get to know

tuesday 14 january
But I want shampoo that volumizes AND strengthens AND moisturizes AND repairs damage AND preserves colour

#FIRST WORLD GIRL PROBLEMS

that person better). Very few hands, if any, are raised. Then I say to the audience, "Stand up if you live in a home that doesn't have a dirt floor." Everyone stands and I explain, "You are now richer than fifty percent of the people in the world." I then ask everyone to continue standing if their home has a window. No one moves. "That now makes you wealthier than sixty-five percent of the people in the world!"

The next challenge I give is to have the group continue standing if they have the opportunity to eat breakfast, lunch, and dinner every day. Everyone usually remains standing, except the women who are dieting in the room. Oh snap! I tell them, "That now makes you richer than eighty percent of the people in the world." When I ask the audience again to raise their hands if they consider themselves to be world-class rich, every single hand in the room goes up. Did their financial circumstances change? No, but their perspective sure did!

We are counseled to "seek not for riches but for wisdom, and behold, the mysteries of God shall be unfolded unto you, and then shall you be made rich. Behold, he that hath eternal life is rich" (D&C 6:7). I like the following poem by an unknown author to help us remember how to balance the value of a buck with the worth of a soul.

Supposing today were your last day on earth,
The last mile of your journey you'd trod.
After all of your struggles, how much are you worth?
How much can you take home to God?

Don't count as possession your silver and gold,
For tomorrow you leave them behind,
And all that is yours to have and to hold
Are the blessings you've given mankind.

Just what have you done as you've journeyed along
That is really and truly worthwhile?
Do you think that your good deeds would offset the wrong?
Can you look o'er your life with smile?

We are only supposing, but if it were real
And you invoice your deeds from your birth
And figure the profits you made in life's deal,
How much are you really worth?

President N. Eldon Tanner said, "I am convinced that it is not the amount of money an individual earns that brings peace of mind as much as it is having *control* of his money. . . . The key to spending less than we earn is simple—it is called discipline" ("Constancy Amid Change," *Ensign*, Nov. 1979).

Finally, we can't leave the topic of money without talking about tithing for a quick second. The Lord is eager to give us blessings when we are obedient to any of His laws. When you pay tithing, however, the blessings aren't always financial. It doesn't mean you're going to suddenly win the lottery. Sometimes the blessing comes in the form of a job so you can *work* to earn more money. My sister's experience is a perfect example.

When she was in graduate school she needed money to pay for college. She also wanted to serve a mission, so the total amount she would need was quite a large obstacle. She obediently paid tithing, so she knew she had the right to ask Heavenly Father for a blessing. Funds were short and she asked Father what she should do. *Work* was the answer! She prayed for help getting a job and the very next day she found one. Then she found another one and then *another* one! She found three part-time jobs that would give her just enough money and some great work experience to put on her résumé. She was willing to do her part and considered the windfall of job opportunities a true miracle. Heavenly Father isn't an ATM. He doesn't give free handouts. We have to do our part first and then the blessings will come. They may not always come that fast, but they *will* come.

FOR THE GUYS' EYES ONLY

Guys, you may have incredible self-control when it comes to saving and spending money. You may be a hard worker and think carefully before making purchases. If, however, you marry a girl who doesn't have the same self-control with money that you have, you could have serious problems in your marriage. Finances, or lack thereof, are the number one cause for divorce. Someone once wisely warned young men, "Whether you end up with a nest egg or a goose egg depends on which chick you marry."

Here are some red flags you need to watch for when you're dating:

- Does your girlfriend want you to call her "Princess"?
- Does your girlfriend carry a tiny dog around in her purse?
- Does your girlfriend have to buy the newest trend to hit stores this week?
- Does your girlfriend drive an expensive car she didn't pay for by herself?
- Does your girlfriend have a thousand pairs of shoes?

If you answered yes to any of those questions, run! Get a new girlfriend, quick! What you have on your hands is a "high maintenance" girl who will spend every dollar you earn. I'm joking . . . but not really.

As for being the "breadwinner" in the family, it is your primary responsibility to provide for your family. Your wife may help you, but her primary calling is to nurture and care for the family. Which would you rather do: bring home the bacon or fry it up in a pan? Mmm . . . bacon . . . "The Family: A Proclamation to the World" outlines these duties. Heavenly Father, in His great wisdom, has divinely created men and women with unique gifts that make this division of labor a blessing to a family.

I have talked to many women who resent their husbands who sit around playing video games when there are bills to pay and money to earn. I've also talked to many parents who are frustrated with their grown sons who are still living at home without any ambition. You really don't want to be *that* guy, living in your mom's basement, eating microwave burritos and surfing the net all day, do you? Be. A. Man.

For the Lasses with Glasses

You might ask the question, "What if I'm a young woman who only wants to get married and be a mom and not have a big career?" Good question. Let me answer it with a few questions of my own:

* What if you never get married?
* What if your husband becomes disabled and can't work?
* What if your husband wants to get a graduate degree and you need to pay the bills while he's in school?
* What if your husband dies young and you have to be the income earner in the family?

In a sense, women have to be even more clever than men. They have to have marketable skills ready to use at any time to earn money while they try to stay at home raising their children. They need to be able to enter the workforce competently at any time.

Once children are in school, you can always work and still get home before the kids get back from school. Find a talent that you love and can develop well enough to earn a little extra money, if necessary, by using or even teaching it. A clever wife can earn extra money by teaching piano lessons, sewing designer curtains, tutoring Spanish, and so on. When money is tight, just try thinking outside the box to find a cheaper way to get what you want. Free is my drug of choice.

Here's an example of what I mean by that. When my husband and I were first married, we wanted to join a nice, but expensive, fitness center near our house. We really loved the posh facilities, but we knew we couldn't afford their monthly fees. I noticed they were short on water aerobics instructors, so I offered to teach some classes in exchange for a free membership for me and my husband. I was thrilled when they offered to pay me for each class *and* gave us free memberships!

No, I had never taught a water aerobics class before, but I was willing to learn and take some certification classes on the weekends. I ended up teaching classes there for almost ten years and my children who were later born also got free memberships! I was able to earn a little bit of extra money, get my whole family free memberships, get paid to work out, get free babysitting for my kids in the fitness center playroom, add experience and management status to my résumé, and keep myself in shape. Sweet!

What if you like exotic, expensive vacations? How about becoming a travel agent? You can save money on your own vacations and even make a little extra on the side! What if you love to go see Broadway shows at the theater, but can't afford those pricey tickets? Did you know you could offer to be an usher for free and then you get to see the show after you've helped people get to their seats? (I used to do that as a pre-teen!)

Think about what it is you want in your life and then find a creative way to make it happen. If you don't go out there and make it happen it may never find its way into your life.

Girls, a lot of wives are the ones in their marriage who balance the checkbook and keep the books. Some girls think that's the guy's job in a marriage. It's unwise to be completely clueless about financial matters. Learn about the stock market, investment properties, treasury bills and economics, all that "boring" stuff. Many wives leave all the bills and finances up to their husbands and then when their husbands die or leave, they are left completely helpless and make foolish decisions with their money. Both husband and wife should take equal responsibility in managing the family finances.

Girls, you have a brain and the Lord expects you to use it.

RANDOM JOKE ABOUT GLASSES

A woman walks into an optometrist's office to return a pair of glasses she purchased for her husband a week ago. The doctor asks, "What seems to be the problem?"

The woman replies, "I'm returning these glasses because my husband still doesn't see things my way."

SUCCESS TIPS FROM MY WISE FRIENDS WHO WORK HARD

* The best place to find a helping hand is at the end of your own arm. —Mary Canale Sanders
* Listen to your mother! —Tera Duncan (She's my big sister and a great mother!)
* If you love what you do, you'll never work a day in your life. —Lucas Worthen (I was his high school Spanish teacher several years ago. He got his pilot's license at age sixteen!)
* Don't despair. It gets better. I promise! —Scott Galet (He and I became great friends in high school when I dated his brother, Bret. After Bret and I broke up, Scott and I kept hanging out together. He's now a high school teacher!)
* Be yourself! Don't be afraid to stand out. You are happiest when you aren't trying to please everyone around you. —Stephanie Stewart

CHAPTER SIX

Groucho Glasses: Humor Is the Sense We All Have in Common

Okay, here are a few jokes to get you started on this chapter:

What do you call cheese that isn't yours? —Nacho cheese

What do you get from a pampered cow? —Spoiled milk

What do prisoners use to call each other? —Cell phones

What do you call Santa's helpers? —Subordinate Clauses

Someone stated that humor is the best sense we have in common. At a fireside I attended many years ago, Lucille Johnson said, "Have you ever read a mortician's manual? It should be required reading! In it, it lists five ways to tell a dead man . . . some of us qualify!" By the way, I have a great knock-knock joke. Okay, you start. Gotcha!

Laughter can be the best medicine and its positive effects on your mind and body are no joke. Scores of hospitals and cancer centers around the United States are taking humor seriously enough to create special rooms, television channels, and libraries dedicated to humor. Even just a smile clinically improves your mood. A cool brain is a happy brain. When you smile you draw more air in through your nostrils and it constricts the blood vessels in your face. That cools the cavernous sinus, which cools the blood flowing to the hypothalamus, which controls the emotions! You don't smile because you're happy—you're happy because you smile!

When I'm angry, I actually try to force my face to smile because I know how powerful the biology is behind a smile. You should see me driving in my car sometimes, completely ticked off at something but smiling like a crazy woman!

Comedian-pianist Victor Borge said, "The shortest distance between two people is a smile" (*Wikiquote*). Laughter is even better than a smile. Twenty seconds of hearty laughter is equal to five minutes of aerobic rowing. Laughter creates "inner jogging." It's a whole lot easier than running around that track at school during gym class.

A good hearty laugh causes a temporary increase in your heart rate and blood pressure. This increases circulation and aids the delivery of oxygen and nutrients to tissues throughout your body. Heavy breathing creates vigorous air exchange in the lungs and disrupts your normal breathing pattern, which increases the amount of oxygen in your blood. All of that is just a complex way of saying that laughing is good for you!

Laughter is usually followed by a sense of relief and relaxation, as if we have "let something out." And I'm not talking about milk coming out of your nose when you laugh really hard. Often with a good laugh, there are tears. Emotional tears of laughter actually contain more protein than tears shed over peeling an onion. It is believed such expression of emotion helps rid the body of some of the biochemical products produced when we are under stress. Research has also shown that laughter can even boost your immune system to fight off colds, flu, and sinus problems! (See cncahealth.com.)

Laughter lifts the spirit and provides an excellent way to connect with other people. Laughing is like changing diapers—it doesn't solve the problem but it makes everything okay for a while!

So what does laughing have to do with your future? Fill your future with lots of it! Surround yourself with people who are upbeat, fun, and allow you to laugh and be yourself. Marry someone who makes you laugh every day. Life gets quite stressful once you are married and have bills to pay, mouths to feed, and diapers to change. You need to be able to laugh until it hurts with your spouse. Life is too hard to take it so seriously.

I love the line in the movie *Who Framed Roger Rabbit?* when Jessica, the gorgeously drawn cartoon character answers the question on everyone's mind: "Why would a beautiful woman who could have any man in the world want to marry such a goofy rabbit?" She says in her sexy, deep voice, "He makes me laugh." I'm certainly no bombshell like Jessica, but I agree. My husband is hilarious and makes me laugh every day.

You may not always be happy, but you can be cheerful. When life seems so hard that it's impossible to smile, just remember the Savior's words: "In the world ye shall have tribulation: but be of good cheer; I have overcome the world" (John 16:33).

Lighten Up!
Sung to the tune "If You're Happy and You Know It."
Susan L. Corpany

When life's got you overrun
Then lighten up!
Think of all the good you've done

And lighten up!
If you're job is just half done and
Your big battles just half won,
Pat yourself on half your back
And lighten up!

If you're feeling loaded down
Then lighten up!
Shrug your shoulders, sing a song,
And lighten up!
With a friend or two beside you
And the Savior's love to guide you
Let some sunshine back inside you
Lighten up!

Here are some suggested uses of laughter for stress management from the book *The Healing Power of Humor* by Allen Klein:

* Listen to tapes of jokes when you know you will have a very stressful drive in the car.
* Keep a cartoon book by the phone to flip through when you get put on hold and want to scream.
* Start a file of good cartoons and jokes to use when needed (on yourself or others!).
* Keep funny mementos around your house to remind you of good times and heartwarming experiences.
* Look for the humor in irony. Accept Murphy's Law. Plan on things going wrong.
* Remember that today's upsets are tomorrow's laughs. Sometimes only a small amount of time will allow you to see the humor in the things that make you nuts.
* Make a point of sharing funny observations with others. Nothing can replace the warmth and camaraderie of the human connection.

I would add to these helpful suggestions to make laughter last. Write down the amusing things that happen to you in your journal or begin a journal that is dedicated just for your life's funny moments. I've kept a special journal for each of my children that contains entries of funny things they have said and done while growing up. One of my boys calls it his "funny book" and loves to read it over and over and laugh at himself.

Groucho Glasses

Surround yourself with humor. Post cartoons on your bathroom mirror, a bulletin board, or the family refrigerator and then change them every so often for all to enjoy. In my formal dining room I have a statue of Michelangelo's famous *David* sitting on a fancy pedestal. To remind myself and visitors that life isn't so serious, *David* is wearing a pair of beach bum sunglasses.

"A merry heart doeth good like medicine: but a broken spirit drieth the bones" (Proverbs 17:22). Get your daily dose of humor so your bones don't get all dried up! Fill your future with lots of bright, happy moments by starting today. Make someone laugh right now. Go ahead, I'll wait while you put this book down for a few minutes.

Who do you know in your life who could use some cheering up?

Write down their names and what you could do to lighten their load:

☀

☀

☀

Have you seriously considered all the possible reasons to the age-old question "Why did the chicken cross the road?" What if the chicken were LDS? Here are some reasons you may not have pondered.

Brigham Young: Because this is the right place in the road.

Martin Harris: I have never denied seeing the chicken cross the road.

Nephi: It is better for a chicken to cross the road than a nation dwindle in unbelief.

BYU president: I'm not so much concerned that the chicken crossed the road, but that its feathers were not knee length.

Lamoni's servants: We don't know why it crossed the road; all we know is its wings had been cut off.

The Doctrine and Covenants: The duty of a chicken is to cross the road when there is no other poultry present.

Noah: Are you sure there weren't two chickens?

Doubting Thomas: I don't really believe the chicken crossed the road.

Laman: To usurp the authority of his older brother chickens and to take possession of their coop.

Elders quorum president: It was the thirty-first and he had to get his home teaching done.

Relief Society president: That's where the refreshments were!

Temple Square tour guide: The acoustics are so good you can hear the chicken cross the road from any seat in the Tabernacle.

Gerald Lund: Not only did this chicken cross the road, but his whole family crossed the road as well. The grand, panoramic story of this chicken's family will be told in my soon-to-be-released thirty-six volume set "The Cluck and the Glory."

FOR THE GUYS' EYES ONLY

Gorgeous women marry average-looking guys for only these reasons:

- He's rich.
- He treats her like a queen.
- He makes her laugh.

A good friend of mine is married to a nice man who is just that: nice. He used to be more carefree and fun when they were dating, but he's too serious all of the time now. If given the choice of having a night out with her girlfriends or staying home with her cranky husband, she says she'd choose the happy company away from him. That's kind of sad, right? Guys, make sure your girl has fun with you.

It is also important to be sensitive to her seemingly erratic moods. My dad was always super sensitive around his three daughters, often bringing us flowers and showing unusual patience. I once asked him how it was that he understood how to act around us when we were "hormonal" or irrational. He said that when he was in high school, he had a girlfriend who was a bubbly cheerleader. Once a month she would become unusually quiet and sad. He didn't quite understand what was happening to her, but he knew it was something significant. Don't worry. I'm not going to go into all the details about why girls become hormonal. Just know that girls deserve your utmost kindness, even when they seem to be going nuts. They probably are, but it's only temporary.

Laugh a lot, but always be mindful of what or who is the brunt of your jokes. Richard L. Evans counseled, "Our character is revealed by what we laugh at" ("The Charted Course of the Church in Education"). Don't be cruel. I always tell my sons, "*Never, ever* make fun of a girl or you'll end up on some Jerry Springer kind of show in ten years where the girl confronts you in front of millions of people on national TV for being a complete jerk." I'm totally serious! What you might think is a funny, little joke could hurt a girl's self-esteem for years. Did you hear me? *Never.*

It's A Poor Joke
Anonymous

When some woman blushes with embarrassment.
When some heart carries away an ache.
When something sacred is made to appear common.
When a man's weakness provides the cause for laughter.
When profanity is required to make it funny.
When a little child is brought to tears.
When everyone can't join in the laughter.

For the Lasses with Glasses

We all have shortcomings and need to be able to laugh at ourselves. Poking fun at yourself lets others know you don't take yourself too seriously, but be careful not to belittle yourself either.

Keep a joy journal and fill it with jokes and happy memories and things that will make you smile when you are feeling down. By the way, it's *normal* to not be happy all the time. Our fluctuating hormones can have a powerful influence on our mood, if you know what I mean. Be gentle with yourself. When I was younger, I noticed a trend every few weeks when I would think irrationally and get very depressed. I soon learned to never make big decisions during "that time." I also stocked up on chocolate. A year's supply—you know, to follow the prophet.

RANDOM JOKE ABOUT GLASSES

What do you call a blind dinosaur?
—Icantseeasaurus

SUCCESS TIPS FROM MY WISE FRIENDS WHO ARE ALSO HILARIOUS

* *Never* eat anything bigger than your head. —Roger Hayes
* Never compare yourself to others. Your life path has been custom cut for you, and only you. Trying to cross onto someone else's road will only make your journey longer and more difficult. Your unique traits, circumstances, personality, and outlook are part of what makes you special. —Nichole Giles (Fantastic author and mother! Check out her blog at www.nicholegiles.blogspot.com.)
* God reaches down to our level and lifts us up to His. —Dawn Norton
* If you work hard and never give up on your dreams and goals, you will find happiness. —Lisa Brereton
* Heavenly Father loves you and knows you by name. Always remember that. Read Joshua 1:1–9. Do your part and He will do His." —Marsha Ward (She's such a sweet person and wonderful author. Take a peek at her website at www.MarshaWard.com.)

CHAPTER SEVEN

Giant Glasses: Mission Possible

I have a pair of those giant, plastic sunglasses that I think represent my mission. Why? Because a mission has blessed my life in a very big way and they have helped me **SEE** the *Son* better. Serving a full-time mission is one way to earn big and long-lasting rewards for a very small investment of time. The average person nowadays lives to be about seventy-five years old. A full-time mission only lasts two years and even less than that for the sister missionaries. Yet the effects and blessings of that short time will be felt throughout your entire life, not to mention eternity.

A mission could be one of the brightest lights in your future that will shine on your life! We are now experiencing the most magnificent wave of missionary work in the history of the world! It's so exciting! It warms my heart and thrills my soul whenever I see the growing number of missionaries entering the MTC each week. I'm one of those blubbering mothers who cries every time I watch a YouTube video of someone receiving their mission call.

I'm also one of those mothers who lives for Mondays. Mondays are the standard P-day (preparation day) when missionaries get time off to write letters home. Each week I receive dozens of letters from my dear young friends who are currently serving missions. By the time this book hits stores, I'll also be receiving missionary letters from one of my own sons! He will be serving in the Nicaragua Mangua North Mission until June 2016! (Tear of happiness . . . sniff.)

I know you've heard many talks and lessons at Church encouraging you to prepare and serve a mission. If you're still debating whether you should go, here are a few more reasons why you should include it in your future:

* You will be a part of God's elite army and be on the front lines of the battle for souls. Cool, right?
* You will come to know the Savior and the Atonement in a very profound way.
* Your understanding of the gospel of Jesus Christ will deepen and fill your soul in ways you never thought possible.
* You'll have two year's worth of funny, awkward stories to tell.
* You will show the Lord that He can count on you.
* You will become a fine instrument to be used by the Lord to find his lost sheep.
* You'll learn how to really hear and live by the Spirit of the Lord.
* You'll gain a thorough knowledge of the gospel.
* You will experience a kind of true joy you have never felt before.
* Bringing souls to Christ hides a multitude of your sins (James 5:20).
* It's a commandment.
* The greatest happiness comes when you forget yourself because you love God more.
* You will gain a better understanding of how the Church works.
* You'll learn how to be a more effective member missionary for the rest of your life.
* You might get to see a cool part of the world and learn a new language!
* You will make new friends that will last a lifetime (your companions, your investigators, and Church members in the areas where you'll serve).
* You will develop a greater understanding of hard work and discipline.
* You will develop a greater appreciation for and testimony of the importance of obedience.
* You will earn the honorable title of "Returned Missionary."
* You will have a sense of pride that you accomplished something very difficult.
* You will learn how to live twenty-four hours a day with a companion, something that will prepare you for marriage.

- According to Joseph Smith, it's the most important work you can do here on earth.
- Father will be disappointed if you return to heaven alone.
- You will have amazing spiritual experiences.
- You will develop spiritual strength that will enrich your marriage and family.
- You will better understand what your own children and grandchildren will go through when they serve missions.
- You will gain wisdom that you cannot learn in any other way.
- You'll always have great material you can use when you're asked to give talks in Church for the rest of your life.
- You will have leadership opportunities that will teach you lessons you can use in your future career.
- Your testimony will touch countless lives as the descendents of the people you teach will bless your name forever.
- Once your investigators are baptized, they will begin to do genealogy and then perform baptisms for their ancestors. Those ancestors will be standing in long lines to thank you when you arrive in heaven!
- You will learn to love like Christ loves. That's one of the most important qualities we're supposed to develop here in mortality!
- People you cared for deeply in the premortal world may be waiting for you to find them and teach the gospel to them here.
- In the famous words of El Esquelto in the movie *Nacho Libre*, "It's like an adventure!"

If you're thinking about serving a mission, go to https://www.lds.org/callings/missionary to learn more about how to prepare and submit your papers. I'm so excited for you!

If you're still unsure, keep reading.

Would you be happy if I gave you a free scoop of ice cream? If you're like me, you're yelling, "Yes, please! Now, please!" as you hold out your hands. How about if I offered you a double scoop? Nice, right? Well, if you like that, how would you feel if I presented you with a gigantic hot fudge ice cream sundae with several scoops of different flavors, yummy toppings, and fresh bananas and strawberries on the side with huge piles of whipped cream and a cherry on top? Now, all you ice cream haters, be quiet and let me make my point. A scoop is great, right? Two scoops make you do the happy dance! But a big sundae is just plain awesome.

Allow me to share with you an example I experienced that illustrates true joy. When I was in high school, my boyfriend Dale joined the Church. What a wonderful scoop of ice cream! It was awesome and delicious to my soul! It was an amazing experience to go through the missionary discussions with him, sit next to him in seminary and church, discover answers to both of our questions, and grow spiritually together. Delicious ice cream. Incomprehensible joy. I highly recommend it!

When Dale turned nineteen, he was called to serve a mission. I was so excited for him and couldn't wait to write to "my" missionary. I was so proud of him and I discovered an increasing amount of joy in reading about his experiences and watching him deepen his understanding of the gospel and love for the Savior while he served his mission. Pass the double scoop of ice cream. I felt more than happiness; I felt an abiding joy that I knew was eternal.

Now, here comes the good part. When Dale was almost finished with his mission, I received a very special letter in the mail. It was from a teenager who had been baptized by Dale. He submitted his own mission papers and had just received a call to serve. In the letter he thanked me for being brave and teaching Dale about the gospel of Jesus Christ when we were teenagers. I cannot even describe the depth of joy I felt to know that my meager missionary efforts with my boyfriend had rippled out to include this stranger who would then go on to teach others. My heart almost burst. That, my dear friends, is a hot fudge sundae.

There is no joy equal to that of bringing others to Christ. As you share the gospel with others, you learn to love them as the Savior does. Remember when Alma and the sons of Mosiah went on missions? Well, of course you don't remember that; you weren't there. Silly goose. Remember reading about their adventures in the Book of Mormon? You can tell they were great missionaries because of the pure love they felt for the people, even for the rotten Lamanites who were so awful to them.

In Mosiah 28:3 it says, "Now they were desirous that salvation should be declared to every creature, for they could not bear that any human soul should perish; yea, even the very thoughts that any soul should endure endless torment did cause them to quake and tremble."

Do you feel that way about people? Even toward the mean and stupid people out there? (There sure are a lot of them out there, right?) You *will* feel that way when you serve a mission. That's the kind of pure love the Savior has and wants us to develop while we're here on earth. In fact, that's one of the biggest lessons we're supposed to learn while we're here. I want to love people like the Savior does. Unfortunately, I can't say that I'm successful at it one hundred percent of the time. Just keep serving others and your capacity to love will grow.

A young friend of mine from New Zealand, Tannar Manuirirangi, is currently serving a mission. In a recent letter he wrote, "I've been thinking a lot lately and I've noticed something. Before my mission, if I saw half of the people I see on my mission, I would have turned my head and walked the other way. On my mission when I see the same exact people, I square my shoulders and I go talk to them. I've been given an opportunity to change my actions and get a second chance on life. As we repent and gain the desire to change, the grace of Christ steps in. Let us have more self-control in every situation we are given and watch the grace and mercy of Christ unfold." Godspeed, Elder!

I served my mission in magnificent Spain and could talk your ear off for hours about everything I learned and did there. It was hard and wonderful. I won't sugarcoat it and tell you a mission is all peachy-dandy, because in reality it's one of the hardest things some people ever do. You'll experience a roller coaster of emotions every day. You'll wear out your shoes from all that walking, as well as your knees from all that praying. You'll feel the need to talk to Heavenly Father almost every moment of the day, which is exactly why missionaries learn what He sounds like and how they grow closer to Him more than ever in their lives.

One morning, the eight of us missionaries who were serving in the same little town gathered to hold our weekly district meeting. We took turns organizing our efforts, sharing spiritual messages, bearing testimony to one another and getting reenergized to go out there and find souls to bring to Christ. We were pretty pumped up and walked out of the church building together, feeling on fire to work hard again. As we walked down the street, one of the missionaries pointed at some people nearby who were oblivious to this powerful team of missionaries in their presence. He proclaimed, "If they really knew who we were, they would come running to us!" Feeling like God's powerful army, the rest of us agreed and patted ourselves on the back for being the Lord's mighty representatives on earth. We whooped and cheered about how great it was to be a missionary and how we were going to baptize the entire country.

Finally, our district leader quietly corrected us with love. He humbly said, "No, you've got it backwards. If we really understood who *they* were, we would be running to them." The group instantly became silent. The truth cut us to our cores. He was right. I'll never forget that moment. It brings tears to my eyes even now. Our duty, our calling, our privilege is to help our dear brothers and sisters come unto Christ. It is an honor to be a part of the Lord's great work.

Come work for the Lord. The work is hard, the hours are long, and the pay is low. But the retirement benefits are out of this world! Check out these helpful websites for missionaries:

- www.mission.net
- http://preparetoserve.com
- www.lds-missions.org (They even have an app!)
- www.ldsmissions.com
- www.ldsmissionblogs.com
- www.ldsmissionarymoms.com (Tell your mom about this site so she can get support from other teary-eyed moms who miss their missionary kids!)

I could write an entire book just of inspiring missionary stories that illustrate how much God loves you and knows you. So many times on my mission I was reminded that it is a privilege to represent the Lord in His work here on earth. One morning my companion and I were standing at a bus stop where several busses were taking people in different directions. We chatted with the people who were waiting and I met a woman who was interested in learning more about the gospel. She wrote down her address and asked us to please visit her later in the afternoon. I put the piece of paper in my coat pocket and then she was swooped off onto a bus to take her to another destination.

My companion and I returned to our apartment for lunch. In Spain the entire country shuts down midday so that families can return home for their largest meal of the day and a little siesta. Nice tradition, eh? After we cleaned up, we headed back out to find that woman's house, but the paper in my pocket had vanished! We searched the entire apartment, thinking it might have fallen out of my pocket when I took my coat off. It was nowhere to be found. We were so discouraged, but we thought we might be able to remember the basic area. We offered a prayer that we would be able to find her and then set off for the neighborhood where she said she lived. We wandered around, hoping the street name would look familiar when we saw it.

Every time we were stumped, we would kneel down in an alley to pray for more guidance and then get a feeling to turn left or right. Finally, we arrived at an old, dirty door that we thought for sure would be hers. We had truly felt guided there. When the door opened, a man saw us and suddenly began to cry. He told us he had been praying for God to send angels to help him and his wife. She was very sick in bed and they knew that God could help. They were new in the town and didn't know anyone. What's amazing is that many years prior, the wife had been baptized into the Church, but she had fallen into inactivity.

The Lord sent us to bring this sweet couple back into the fold. What a humbling feeling to be those angels someone was praying for. If the Lord knows a brokenhearted, humble man with an old, dirty door somewhere in Spain, He certainly knows you too. So, what ever happened to that lady we met at the bus stop? We never found her. Maybe *she* was the angel who was sent to make sure we found that man and his wife.

One year at Christmastime my entire zone was gathered for a special Christmas dinner and gift exchange. I was in the kitchen washing dishes when I noticed a bunch of the missionaries huddled together, laughing and listening intently to a cassette player. I didn't want to miss out on the action and wondered what they were hearing with such big smiles on their faces, since we were only allowed to listen to the Mormon Tabernacle choir and hymns. One of the missionaries had written and recorded a "Joseph Smith Rap" before his mission and was sharing the music with the other elders.

This was back in the late '80s when rap was still pretty new, so everyone thought this new style of sharing the Prophet Joseph's story was pretty funny.

The music was catchy and the message was what we taught in our first discussion to investigators. I loved it! I asked the elder for a copy and he handed me a cassette. Wow, cassette—crazy, right?

The next day my companion and I were tracting in an apartment building when a teenage boy opened the door. He said he wasn't interested in talking about religion, but he thought it was cool that I was from America. We learned that he was the second-best break-dancer in all of Spain and that it was his dream to go to America and compete with the break-dancers there. I asked him to show me his sweet moves and he began spinning around on the floor. Wait! Suddenly, I remembered I still had that missionary's rap tape in my bag! I asked my new young friend if he would like to break dance to my music. He was excited to hear it and showed off some more of his fancy moves while it played.

When the music ended, he asked me to translate the English words. Bingo! The first discussion! I would play a part of the tape and then explain Joseph's experience in the Sacred Grove. By the time the tape was over, the boy had just heard about the First Vision. He stopped dancing and then quietly said, "Again." This time he didn't dance, but instead he listened with real intent. It was a magical moment as we felt the Spirit wash over him and testify of truth. What a miracle to have the very tool in my bag that would touch this teenager's heart in such a unique way.

The Lord's hand is in every detail of this work. You will be privileged to see *many* miracles when you serve as a missionary. If you *want* to see miracles, serve a mission. Of course, Heavenly Father could part the Red Sea and convert thousands at a time (oh yeah, He already did that), but He touches one heart at a time, one soul at a time, because each person is so important to Him.

Please know that wherever you get called to serve a mission, that is exactly where Heavenly Father needs you. My oldest son had been called to serve a mission in Argentina, but something had postponed his visa from arriving on time while he was in the MTC. He was told he would have to go to Maryland for a couple of weeks while he waited for the right paperwork. He was anxious to get to Argentina and a little disappointed about the delay, but he obediently went to Baltimore where he stayed in a super ghetto apartment with the missionaries who were serving in the inner city there. He loved it and thought it was hilarious that police detained him and his new companion one day because they were the only white guys riding on a bus and the passengers were afraid they were dangerous spies or something.

He had some fun experiences there, but it wasn't until he began teaching a certain black man that he remembered he had dreamed about this man several months before he received his mission call to Argentina. He was teaching this man the gospel in his dream, but once he was called to Argentina he dismissed it from his mind because he didn't think there were black people in that country. While my son was teaching this dear investigator, the man shared with him that he had also had a dream about my son and knew that if he ever met him that he was supposed to pay close attention to the important message. My son knew that he was exactly where the Lord wanted him. Two weeks later he flew off to Argentina, forever grateful for the time he was able to spend in his detoured city.

One time on my mission I was transferred to a new city and was a bit sad to leave my last area where I had met some wonderful investigators and members of the Church. When I arrived at church in my new area to meet the members of the branch, I was so excited to see familiar faces! I immediately approached an older couple that I knew. They greeted me with open arms and it was an unexpected, happy reunion. As we chatted, we tried to remember when it was we last saw each other. An odd feeling overcame us when we couldn't remember how we knew each other. But we *did* know each other. Tears of joy fell down our cheeks as we realized that it wasn't here on earth where we had met. When we first saw each other in the small Spanish chapel that day, we had been given a brief remembrance of heaven where we first met.

Finally, I hope you know that you don't have to wear a black name tag in order to do missionary work. The most effective missionaries are the ones who share the gospel their entire lives. Open your mouth and start sharing what you know and how it has blessed your life! When I served a mission, the statistics showed that for every one hundred doors we knocked on, one person would join the Church. *But* if a member of the Church referred a friend to us, one out of every three would join! That's a huge difference! I doubt that statistic has changed much over the years. Missionary work has always been so much more successful when the members of the Church get involved.

Write a list of people you know who might actually accept a Book of Mormon from you if you handed them one:

- ✳
- ✳
- ✳
- ✳

If that sounds too scary, write a list of friends who might accept an invitation to go to a fun Church activity with you. It can be playing basketball inside the Church building, a combined youth activity, or even just hanging out with a bunch of Mormon kids.

Giant Glasses

There are other ways you can do missionary work too. For example, pray for missionaries by name. Who are the missionaries serving *from* your ward right now? What are the names of the missionaries serving *in* your ward right now?

Write down their names so you can include them in your prayers:

*

*

*

Missionaries live for letters and care packages. It's such a simple thing you can do to encourage and inspire them. It almost doesn't matter what you say in your letters, missionaries are just thrilled to know that someone is thinking of them while they're far away from home. Try to write positive things that won't get them homesick. They especially love to hear how *you* are sharing the gospel with friends back at home! Check out www.DearElder.com. You can send free snail-mail letters to most of the missions in the world by using their free service! Ask the missionaries you write to if they know of any other missionaries who aren't getting much mail or support and then write to them too!

FOR THE GUYS' EYES ONLY

Just go. The Lord has invited you to go. He is expecting you to go. He needs you to go. I *promise* that you will never regret it.

For the Lasses with Glasses

What about marriage? Who ever said you can't do *both*? For goodness's sake, it's only eighteen months! That may sound like forever to you, but when you're older you'll realize how fast that time flies by in the blink of an eye.

When I was nine or ten years old, a returned sister missionary spoke in sacrament meeting. I had never seen one before. I don't think I even realized they existed. I was fascinated and instantly impressed as she shared her missionary stories with the congregation. I knew right then and there that I wanted to serve a mission. I wanted to be a returned missionary and be like her. Her testimony was so strong and her love seemed so pure and without end. I was ready to pack my bags and go right away. Imagine how discouraged I felt when I learned I had to wait until I was twenty-one years old! Now all of you wonderful girls get to go when you're nineteen! That's fantastic!

Remember when I told you that my dad refused to allow me and my sisters to do anything until after we had graduated from college? Well, I was just about ready to graduate from BYU (Go Cougars!) when I turned in my mission papers. I was so excited to finally be able to go! I'll never forget standing at the gate at the airport to fly to the MTC when my boyfriend, Tom, said, "I can't believe you're really leaving." I looked at his sad face and said, "Um . . . yeah . . . I've been talking about going on a mission ever since I was a little girl!" He and I had been dating for about a year and we were getting serious. I had talked about going on a mission with every boyfriend I ever had; it was definitely not a secret to any of them. I joked and asked, "Well, why didn't you make me a better offer?" He quietly said, "Because I knew you'd say no." He was right.

Tom and I *had* talked about getting married, but we both knew that I wanted to go on a mission *too*. Why couldn't I do *both*? I figured that if he married somebody else while I was gone, then that would mean there was somebody else out there *better* for me! If he was still around when I got back, then he really was "the one" and we'd get married. How could I lose? I thought I had a pretty mature attitude about it, if I do say so myself. Guess what? Tom and I have now been married for twenty-six years. Okay, girls, everyone say in unison, "Awww."

Did I miss him while I was on my mission? Of course. Did I worry that he would marry someone else? Sometimes. Am I glad I went on a mission? *Absolutely*! Has it blessed my marriage? Definitely!

Now, after having said all that, there is nothing wrong with you girls if you choose *not* to serve a full-time mission. I'm completely biased and want you to have that incredible experience, but I know that it's not required. You may choose to get married first and serve a mission later in life with your husband. You may also feel the Lord leading you to pursue another path. That's okay too. Counsel with the Lord in prayer to find out what He wants you to do and then do *that*!

Giant Glasses

RANDOM JOKE ABOUT GLASSES

What did the sailor say to the captain who wore glasses?

—Eye-Eye Captain

SUCCESS TIPS FROM MY WISE FRIENDS WHO ARE CURRENTLY SERVING MISSIONS ALL OVER THE WORLD

* Forget about labels and the expectations of other people. Choose what will make the Lord happy, and you'll discover that most happiness comes that way to you. —Steven Duncan (He's my *amazing* nephew

who is serving his mission in Siberia. Yep, they actually send missionaries there! He'll be home April 2015.)

- Sometimes we don't always understand the whys or the hows, but Heavenly Father knows *exactly* who you are and who you can become. Everything suddenly becomes very clear as we trust enough to take the little steps of faith toward him. —Keaton Hawker (He's a cool missionary from my ward who is serving in Frankfort, Germany, on his mission.)
- If you want to be happy in life, obey the commandments, not just the commandments you like or are easy to follow but *all* the commandments. —Alexandria Clawson (She is currently serving in the Argentina Buenos Aires South Mission, and her brother is serving in the Argentina Buenos Aires North Mission! Isn't that awesome?)
- The more I understand that God *wants* to be a part of our daily life, I'm more careful to *allow* Him into mine. —Tanner Long (He's one of the most talented, funny guys I know, and he's my nephew! He just got back from serving his mission in Chile, close to where David Archuleta served his mission!)
- I think some of the best advice would just be follow the commandments, really simple. My mission president's wife told us once that God has been creating the earth for over 13.3 billion years! That's a ton of time! And from the beginning of time, He gave us commandments, basic laws that haven't changed! So if He has been doing it for 13.3 billion years, let's trust that He's got it right and He knows what He's talking about! We have to stop trying to change His rules, His laws, and instead live them and submit our will to His. That's when we find true happiness! —Elizabeth Thompson (She is currently serving a mission in Cuzco, Peru. That's where the emperor got his groove.)
- I think the greatest thing we can do to be happy and successful is to "turn our arrows out" and to focus on others! We all need to count our blessings and notice the goodness of a loving Heavenly Father all around us. We need to focus on those things that matter most and prioritize our time accordingly. —Gracie Platt (She is the most adorable missionary ever and is serving in Birmingham, Alabama, right now! She always says, "I'm so obsessed with being a missionary!" Her father and my husband were missionary companions—twice!)

- The only advice I have for the youth is to study, understand, and implement the Atonement of Jesus Christ into your life every single day. Do not let a day go by without humbly thanking the very perfect being who descended below all for you, your friends' and family's salvation. The Atonement will unleash the power intended to live according to the will of God, and once you are on God's path, your light is ever so bright that the chains of hell will have no power over you. The Atonement was specifically done for you and me. If we aren't willing to implement all that we can from the Atonement, then we need to reevaluate our obedience. Our obedience is an example of our love toward the Savior. The Atonement is the most important thing I could offer the youth of this day, and obedience tied hand-in-hand with that. Obedience brings freedom. Obedience to the gospel brings celestial glory and heavenly guidance! —Tannar Manuirirangi (Tanner is currently serving in Salt Lake City, Utah! Yes, that's an actual place where you might get called to serve your mission. You could actually go tracting in the prophet's neighborhood!)
- Have fun with the Spirit! Trust God. He is your friend! Things will work out in the end! —Michael Grogitsky (He joined the Church as a teenager and is currently serving a mission in Seattle, Washington!)
- The best way to do really great things is slowly and steadily. No one starts out on top. You have to start slow, build a base, get the basics down, move and do it again. Something that I've seen a lot of is people who want to move up faster than they can, but they haven't built a foundation yet. For example, they want to be a leader before they can follow. —Mason Parkes (Mason is from my home ward and is serving in the Mexico Monterrey West Mission!)
- Don't be afraid to ask for help with anything, from the smallest troubles to the biggest sins. The Lord will always help you. You just have to be willing to ask Him for it. —Benny Yamagata (Benny joined the Church in his teens and is now serving in the Korea South Mission until January 2016! He loves it when I call him "Benny Boo." Well, maybe not. But I still call him that anyway.)

CHAPTER EIGHT

Magnifying Glass: See the World Up Close!

There's a whole world out there! Don't you want to see it? It's really awesome! I know way too many adults who say they want to travel . . . someday. With bills to pay and life getting in the way, someday never comes for them. Make plans to travel and have amazing moments in your life now! Create memories. Enjoy all there is that's offered in this mortal experience. You'll need to put on those aviator glasses as you jet around the world in your future! (I'm working pretty hard to establish this sunglasses theme for the book.)

Where are some places in the world that "call" to you? Where would you like to visit?

*

*

*

Start learning about those places and actually research how you can go there! For example, did you know that the Church offers a life-changing summer program called Humanitarian Experience for Youth in exotic locations such as Africa, Fiji, Belize, Tonga, Peru, Brazil, and more? Your testimony and muscles will be strengthened as you do humanitarian projects abroad and serve as Christ did. Go to www.hefy.org for more information and an application.

BYU–Idaho has a summer outdoor program called Adventure for Youth, which is a week full of new experiences like white-water rafting, ropes courses, barn dances, horseback riding, and a giant Slip 'N Slide, in addition to the spiritual devotionals and fun friendships you'll enjoy. To learn more about it, go to http://www.byui.edu/outdoor-learning-center/adventure-for-youth-afy/afy-activities.

Have you ever been to the East Coast of the United States? It's gorgeous and super lush and green. (I live in the middle of the desert in Las Vegas right now so green is a big deal for me.) Southern Virginia University is a small LDS college that hosts summer youth sessions on their campus.

Check out www.svu.edu/efy. One of the best things about the East Coast is the fireflies! It's like being at Disneyland at night with all of the magical lights! I figure it's God's way of apologizing for the humidity out there. One of my sons attended the EFY in Nauvoo and got to see all of the Church sites out there. Wonderful!

How about going to a For the Strength of Youth session this summer in Europe! Go to https://www.fsy-europe.org/ to check it out.

Find out if your high school participates in a Foreign Exchange program or consider hosting an international student in your own home next school year. Do you know if there are foreign exchange students in your school? Have you ever introduced yourself to them? Imagine how lonely they must feel so far away from their home and family. They could always use another friend and would love to tell you about their country. There is so much we can learn from one another!

CHEAP ENTERTAINMENT TIP

Do a YouTube search with keywords like "taste American candy" or "taste American food for the first time" and you'll find all kinds of super funny videos of foreigners tasting our food and describing how weird they think it is.

When I was in high school, I was an exchange student in Mexico. I had been to Tijuana for a day with my dad when I was younger and discovered the fun dance of bargaining with the locals for useless junk, but I had never lived in a foreign country before. My exchange trip was just for the summer months because I didn't want to leave my family for an entire school year.

I stayed with a wonderful family in Culiacan, Sinaola, in Mexico. My Mexican "father" had lost his arm just above the elbow, so he would often rest his "nub" on my shoulder because he thought it was hilarious to watch me squirm. I had never lived with anyone who was missing a body part! He was really funny and made me laugh every day. You know how they spell laughing in Spanish? *Ja ja.*

One night my exchange sister and her boyfriend set me up with their friend to go on a double date. The boy was a true gentleman and tried to walk on the outside of the sidewalk to protect me from cars on the street. (Guys, did you know that was a thing? Yep, you're supposed to do that to be chivalrous. Girls will be impressed.) Unfortunately, I didn't know that at the time.

It was a hot summer night, which meant cockroaches were everywhere. You could hear their little bodies crunch as the cars drove over them on the streets. Super gross. As I hopped around the sidewalk trying to dodge the disgusting insects in my path, I didn't realize that my poor date was edging closer and closer on to the street and in the way of oncoming traffic. He was trying so hard to be a gentleman! Poor guy. I was so oblivious. During those months I finally learned to be more aware of others, as well as how to behave properly in another country and culture.

It's hard to decide what you want to do with the rest of your life when you have hardly lived yet! Choosing a college major was really hard for me because I didn't even know what all of my options were. Living abroad introduced me to so many new things and ideas. I felt like my eyes were just opening for the first time. I was tasting the world and thought it was delicious! I can never get enough of exploring new cities and countries.

Your perspective will change when you reach outside yourself and see how others live and think. I dated a boy in high school whose parents were from England and Ireland. They had super cute accents and were delightful to be with. His dad had a worm farm in the backyard. Weird, right? One day we watched a comedy show from England together at his house. I was surprised his family laughed hysterically at something I thought was really dumb. I never realized until then that different cultures have a different sense of humor.

When I went on a BYU Study Abroad program in college, I learned that different cultures think and see the world differently than we Americans do. That was a surprising revelation for me. There is so much to learn!

Generally speaking, you aren't learning much when your mouth is moving. There is something you can learn from *everyone*. Always look for the good in everyone, even that dumb guy you sit next to in third period class. Even *he* can teach you *something* if you look hard enough. Don't dismiss people because they look or act or talk differently from you.

When I was at BYU I lived in the "Spanish House" and attended a student ward with all of the other language houses scattered around town. Now there is an entire apartment complex dedicated just to the language ward near campus! In order to live in the Spanish House, I had to agree to only speak Spanish inside the home. It was a fantastic way to speed up the learning process, but you can probably imagine how quiet it often was inside as we were all trying to learn to speak the language.

The cool part of our student ward was that everyone was learning a different language, so our sacrament meeting hymns sounded like the Day of Pentecost with everyone singing different words. Our Sunday School lessons also had a unique aspect. In the language ward, students would compare their language and cultural understanding to the topic of the day. For example, how many times have you sat through a lesson at church on prayer or even family home evening? About a thousand times, right? In the language ward we talked about what specific words to use when you approach Deity. For example, in Spanish you pray to God in the informal conjugation form: "tu," which is the same form you would use when speaking to a close friend. In Japanese you approach Heavenly Father in the very most respectful, formal manner, as if you were talking to a king. Having Sunday School class discussions like that really added depth to our lessons that helped me understand the gospel in an expanded way. I loved it!

Fill your future discovering all of the beauty the Lord has created for you to enjoy!

FOR THE GUYS' EYES ONLY

If you can learn another language, put that skill on your resume. Employers often want to hire people who can speak to another population as future customers. Whether you take three years of French in school or you teach yourself sign language by watching YouTube videos, develop skills so you can truly communicate with others to improve your hiring potential, as well as share the gospel.

For the Lasses with Glasses

You are a cute, young girl, so be mindful of your safety when you travel. Pay attention to what's going on around you rather than focusing on your cell phone or disappearing into your earplugs. The world is fascinating and exciting, but it can also be dangerous if you're not being careful.

Many years ago I was traveling with a bunch of students in Morocco. The leaders cautioned the girls to stay close to the boys because kidnapping was well-known in the area. I naively wandered into an open-air market without a buddy and got absorbed in looking at all of the cool merchandise. (I have Shiny Object Syndrome.) Suddenly, I got a strange feeling that I should look up. I saw two scary-looking men walking toward me and then I realized none of my friends were nearby. I immediately dropped the item I was holding in my hands, quickly slipped under a tent flap, and ran down the dirt path until I saw the student group walking around a corner. It was kind of scary and I'm sure I looked like a crazy person. It reminded me to be smarter about my enthusiasm for exploring strange places. That's all I'm saying—just be careful and smart. The world is an exciting place!

RANDOM JOKE ABOUT GLASSES

A Russian patient went to have his eyes tested. The eye test read, "N Y X C S F R U Z." The optometrist asked, "Can you read any of those letters?" "Read it?" the Russian patient answered, "I know him!"

SUCCESS TIPS FROM MY WISE FRIENDS WHO HAVE FUN ADVENTURES

- Find an adventure in everything you do. —Chris Monahan (This guy is hilarious and has the most amazing missionary stories. One such story is when some bad guys were chasing him and his companion with machetes in the Philippines. Suddenly, the scumbags dropped their weapons and ran away. Surprised and confused, Chris and his companion walked to a nearby house to find refuge. The bad guys followed them to the house and pounded on the door yelling, "We're not afraid of you anymore. Now you don't have those soldiers to protect you!" It was then that the missionaries realized the Lord had sent protective soldiers to stand by them when the bad guys were going to do them harm. While the elders hadn't seen their protectors, the bad guys did! Isn't that awesome?)
- Be your best self. —Kathleen Larkin Wardle
- Rise above your circumstances. Change the world one person at a time, starting with you, and be the inspiration you've been searching for. —Lindsey Stirling (If you haven't already discovered her, run to her YouTube channel right now! She's fantastic!)
- *Can't* is not part of our vocabulary. *Try* and *do* will take you where you want to go. —Sheila Windley Staley
- Create a bucket list and start checking things off it today. Dream big. Live big. —Jennifer Jackson

CHAPTER NINE

Prescription Glasses: Improving Your Eternal Vision

The closer I got to my fortieth birthday, the more I kept rubbing my eyes and wondering why I couldn't see well anymore. I thought *old* people needed glasses. My twin sister mentioned that she had recently bought a new set of prescription glasses because she noticed her vision wasn't as good as it used to be. Well, that explained it. *She* was old, not me!

What do prescription glasses do? Besides making someone feel self-conscious, they actually help people who have less than perfect vision to **SEE** better. You need to get them from a certified eye doctor. The Lord has been called the "Great Physician" and He has given us a type of prescription glasses too—our patriarchal blessings! Patriarchal blessings help us to **SEE** better and clearer too! Our Heavenly Father has the best vision because He knows who we *really* are. He knew us before we came here to earth and He is the Father of our spirits.

No two people are exactly alike, so prescription glasses are never the same. Neither are patriarchal blessings. The Lord knows what our strengths and weakness are. He expects us to accomplish certain things, given those circumstances and conditions. I'm an identical twin and can tell you that even we see differently sometimes.

We're all different with unique talents and challenges. You can't use someone else's prescription or else you can damage your eyes. Stop comparing yourself to other people! We see people's "Sunday best" and often don't know the whole story of what happens to them during the rest of the week. We often feel inadequate around other members of the Church because we think they are perfect and we know how we are not! To others, *you* may seem perfect! We need to be careful not to judge others. There will always be people who are better than you are at doing certain things, but there will also be people who are worse than you are. Concentrate on what makes you unique, and stop comparing yourself!

An Original
Susan L. Corpany

You are an original work of art,
Not a carbon copy that can't be told apart
From others of its kind that stand upon a shelf.
So why don't you start to realize the value of yourself.

Many a high price is paid for something that is rare,
Something no one else has got, not here or anywhere.
A woman may buy herself a gorgeous, costly gown,
Yet may run into its double in her travels about town.

But one thing you can be sure that you will never do
Walking down the street is meet another you.
No one else can do the things you were put here to do.
No one else looks at things with your same point of view.

No one else can touch the people you were meant to touch.
You are an original and worth so very much.
So when you feel a tendency to mark your price tag down,
Remember that another you is nowhere to be found.

Heavenly Father sees things how they *really* are. That's why touching base with Him in daily prayer is so important to keep an eternal perspective! He knows what will make us truly happy. He knows what our futures *can* be and He gives us a lot of hints and information in our patriarchal blessings. If you haven't received your patriarchal blessing yet, get one! If you already have one, read it often.

Evaluate yourself to see how you are doing. Some of the things you

Prescription Glasses

may find in your blessing are special talents you have been given by a loving Heavenly Father; accomplishments you had in the premortal world; covenants you made with Father; future blessings He wants to give you; and of course your lineage, which links you with valiant saints and, through such bonds, identifies your inherent responsibilities and blessings.

sunday 10 november
GREAT
OUTFIT
STATS
accessory compliments from friends : 1
outfit compliments from strangers : 3
boys who go out of their way to talk to me : 2
new friends : 3
never happens
probably not related to my outfit

Your patriarchal blessing is not like a fortune cookie or gypsy reading. The promised blessings you read about on paper are blessings predicated upon your faithfulness. What does that mean? They only come true if you are true.

Some things in my patriarchal blessing have already been fulfilled, like the promise of indescribable joy while serving a full-time mission. I served a full-time mission in Spain and can't even begin to tell you how wonderful the joy when I pondered the fact that I was a part of God's army right there on the front lines! It was incredible! No feeling can compare with helping people discover the Lord and His gospel, and then watching them enter into the waters of baptism. It's awesome! I thought that when I returned home that particular part of my blessing would be completed. Not so. Years later when my mission president had just been called as a General Authority in the Church, we had a special reunion. The room was filled with the

Spirit, and the joy I felt that night was truly indescribable. The blessings from my service as a missionary keep coming.

Other parts of my blessing I'm still waiting to see happen. Maybe they will happen in this life or maybe after I pass through the earthly veil to the other side. Studying your patriarchal blessing frequently, especially in times of important decisions or trials or depression, will quickly remind you and give you the vision of who you really are and what your relationship with God is, and especially what His will for you is. It can comfort you when you feel unloved, unworthy, inadequate, or forgotten. It can point you toward your own special purpose in life.

Prepare yourself spiritually before you get your patriarchal blessing through fasting and prayer. When you talk with Heavenly Father about what special counsel you hope to receive in your blessing, ask specific questions. That helps you to identify what it is you really want to learn from Him, as well as recognize when your question is answered. Tell him your concerns and thoughts. Ask him to reveal answers. He most likely won't tell you your future wife or husband's name though, so don't even bother asking that question! My blessing addressed specific questions in my heart that I had been praying about. The stake patriarch didn't know my questions when he uttered those answers in my blessing. He was simply the mouthpiece, but I know those answers came directly from the Lord! Pretty doggone cool.

Write down what you would like to know from your Father in Heaven about . . .

Your family:

Your future spouse:

Your children:

School:

Work:

Talents:

Your mission on earth:

Friends:

What makes you unique:

How you can build the kingdom of God on earth:

While the patriarch is giving you your blessing, it is being recorded. It is then typed in duplicate; one copy is sent to you in a few weeks, and another is sent to the Church archives. On the day you receive your blessing you might want to record in your journal the impressions and feelings you had of the event. When your copy of the blessing comes in the mail, read it often! The direction a patriarchal blessing provides, in addition to declaring lineage, is a guidepost to living righteously and helping us keep an eternal perspective on our existence here on earth. Like a good set of prescription glasses, your patriarchal blessing can help you **SEE** better!

Just like prescription glasses, your patriarchal blessing is meant just for you. It is not to be shared with everyone. It is a sacred, intimate blessing from the Lord to you to help you keep your life on track and fulfill the mission here that you alone can do. It is to correct and improve *your* vision, not your sister's or your best friend's. It's wise not to compare the contents of your blessing with other blessings and not to share it with just anyone.

Although your blessing is confidential and sacred, it may be shared with members of your family who may be in a position to provide insight, encouragement, or guidance with respect to your blessing. Elder James E. Faust reminds us, "A patriarchal blessing is very personal but might be shared with close family members" ("Patriarchal Blessings," *New Era*, Nov. 1982, 4). It is kind of an LDS tradition to have your parents go with you to get your patriarchal blessings. My parents were not active in the Church when I got mine, so they didn't come with me.

When my boyfriend joined the Church in his teens, he was the only member of the Church in his family, so he asked me to share that moment with him. When my sons received their blessings, our entire family was there for them. I love the idea that all of us in my family know how special each other is. I think it's sometimes helpful for siblings, who can often drive each other nuts, to remember one another's patriarchal blessings and see each other through Heavenly Father's eyes.

Normally it would not be appropriate to read, quote, or discuss your blessing outside your immediate family. However, there may be times when you feel impressed by the Spirit to refer to a particular part.

Joseph F. Smith said, "Such a blessing, given in the spirit of a father's love, and sealed upon us in the authority of the priesthood, becomes a power in our lives; a comfort to our days. It is a message, which if read and honored aright, will become an anchor in stormy days, our encouragement in cloudy days. It states our certain destination here and hereafter, if we live by the law; and as life goes on, it strengthens our faith and leads us into truth." (*Old Testament Student Manual*)

RANDOM THOUGHT ABOUT A PROPHET

Joseph F. Smith was the only son of Hyrum Smith (Joseph Smith's brother). He later became the sixth president of the Church and received the revelation of the redemption of the dead that we know today as Doctrine and Covenants section 138.

The experience of receiving a patriarchal blessing is a blessing itself. You will learn firsthand how important and wonderful and unique you are in the Lord's eyes. Like your earthly parents, your Father in Heaven knows you and loves you, and He expects great things from you. If you haven't received your patriarchal blessing yet, you might want to talk to your parents and bishop to help you determine when the right time is and to help you prepare spiritually to receive it. Your bishop can walk you through the process of how to get one.

Your spiritual ears should be mature enough to hear what the Lord has to say. There is no set age recommended by the Church. However, the person should be able to understand the history and blessings of ancient Israel and have a desire to know the will of God and follow His commandments.

Because of the spiritual nature of the blessing, you might want to fast and pray, study the scriptures, and talk to others about how they draw close to the Holy Ghost. If you feel unworthy, become worthy! Your bishop and parents can help you. Put your life in order now so you will have a future you can look forward to and a past you can be proud of.

If you have already received your patriarchal blessing, what have you learned about yourself?

Write down specific things the Lord told you about . . .

Your gifts:

Your responsibilities:

Challenges you will face:

Counsel you need to follow:

Things you have to look forward to:

The Self We Want To Be
Susan L. Corpany

If we but shape our destiny,
We can become the self we want to be,
Not driven by whim, nor base desire,
But by the inner soul's Celestial fire.

For there lies within our inner spirit,
A still small voice, if we'll but hear it.
Its purpose is to guide aright,
To bless with wisdom, truth, and light.

We dull that voice by sinful ways,
By pride of heart and worldly praise,
By seeking pleasures of the flesh,
Entwining our souls in Satan's mesh.

We tune our inner souls to God
By holding to the Iron Rod

And as we sorrow much for sin,
Behold, the voice of God beams in
To gently lead us with His sheep,

To green pastures and peaceful sleep,
Where all may learn His saving grace.
And meet our Savior face to face.

What joy, what joy will then be ours,
When we are freed from Satan's powers
To shape our lives eternally
Toward God's highest destiny.

RANDOM JOKE ABOUT GLASSES

A man went to an eye specialist to get his eyes tested and asked, "Doctor, will I be able to read after wearing glasses?"

"Yes, of course," said the doctor.

"Oh! Great!" said the patient. "I never learned how to read!"

SUCCESS TIPS FROM MY WISE FRIENDS WHO ARE SIMPLY AWESOME

- You can lead a horse to water, but a pencil must be lead. —Roger Hayes (He's a funny guy, right? Every Halloween he turns his house into a massive haunted house. Check it out at www.HayesHaunt.com.)
- Avoid taking advice from anyone who isn't already where you want to be in life. —Nathan Grant
- Ether 12:27 is a great scripture. Lots of teenagers are at that time in their lives when they're self-conscious about their weaknesses and insecurities, but all you really need is faith in Heavenly Father and He will turn those weaknesses into strengths. Once that faith is there, teens can see their full potential and they can do amazing things in the world. —Crista Guthrie (She performed in the Freshman Orientation talent show at BYU–I, along with one of my sons. She and I became instant friends and I am constantly amazed at her violin talents. Check out her music at: http://noisetrade.com/cristaguthrie.)

Prescription Glasses

* Our symbol of courage in today's world is to live a virtuous life, sincerely respecting the sanctity of life, our bodies, and our relationship to our Father in Heaven. We can trust His timing. We can rely on His promises. Standing together in the strength of the Lord, we can shape the world in preparation for the great and important days ahead. —Fay Klingler (She is such a kind woman who writes a lot of books for LDS girls. One of them is her newest book *We Are Strong!* which you can check out at www.fayklingler.com.)

CHAPTER TEN

3-D Glasses: Step into the World

Have you ever watched a movie in 3-D that was done so well you felt like you were actually inside the movie? I'm a huge movie fan and write reviews at (my shameless plug) www.MovieReviewMaven.blogspot.com. I get a real kick out of those 4-D movies even more. While you're watching a fun flick, your chair rumbles, things drop from the ceiling, and air bursts at your feet. I even saw a 4-D movie where they perfectly timed a string of air to blow across the audience's feet as a bunch of rats were running across the screen. Ick. So fun. I love being in the thick of the action.

Why do I bring this up? Because some of your parents and church leaders are worried that you're living in a 2-D world on your cell phone and missing out on the real world. I'll never forget a Young Women's activity that I had spent many hours planning with the idea that the girls would get to know each other better and would create eternal bonds. It was a Progressive Christmas dinner where we were supposed to sing Christmas carols from house to house as we enjoyed a different dinner course in each beautifully decorated home on our wintery route. I was shocked when all of the girls arrived at the first house, sat on the couch, and then immediately pulled out their cell phones to text other friends. What was even crazier is when we found out that two of the girls were texting each other while they sat right next to each other! Seriously?

3-D Glasses

I remember hearing Jason Wright, the author of the fantastic novel *Christmas Jars*, speak at a Time Out for Women session. He held his new iPhone lovingly in his had and said, "You complete me." He was joking, of course, but I know that some people really do feel more connected to their technology than to real people.

Technology is awesome. I get it. I love it too. You are so lucky to have it at your age. I'm not ancient, but I actually had to type my school papers on a typewriter. I can still smell the white-out liquid I would have to smear on the paper to cover up my typing mistakes. Wow, I just read that sentence out loud and realized I'm practically a dinosaur. I was visiting my sister-in-law's house last summer and helping my son get settled in the guest bedroom when I noticed an antique typewriter on display in the corner. I asked him if he knew what it was. He said no. I'm a *Tyrannosaurus rex*.

Your parents are partly jealous that you get to have all the cool techno gear at your age that they didn't, but they're also annoyed. You often ignore them because you're glued to your cell phone. They're worried that you'll get sucked into your devices and never come back. They're worried that you won't know how to communicate with other human life forms, and that you'll be the geeky kid who can't utter a coherent sentence anymore, and that all of the other adults will laugh at them for their terrible parenting skills.

They're concerned that you haven't learned proper manners, like looking people in the eye when they speak to you or not using your cell phone at the dinner table. They're afraid you're turning into a zombie and can't function without technology. I have a son who would actually curl into the fetal position whenever we would take away his computer. He didn't even know what to do with himself. Parents worry. That's what parents do. That's why they get paid the big bucks to be your parents. That was a joke—your parents don't get paid a penny to raise you.

By the way, when you text, ask yourself, "What would my parents think if they saw what I just wrote?" I would suggest "What would Jesus text?" but you and I both know the cell phone coverage back then was really spotty. You should never text anything that you would be embarrassed for your bishop to see either.

Pay attention to the language used in texts you receive. One of my sons was dating a sweet, nonmember girl from school. She was always very polite and well-mannered around me, and they had a nice friendship. My son even took her to several church events and started teaching her about the gospel. I always do random checks of texts on my kids' cell phones and so I was satisfied that their conversations were innocent and appropriate.

One day I noticed that her language changed dramatically. My son said he didn't know what was going on, but that her behavior was also changing. She had gotten involved with a different crowd at school and was headed in a bad direction. The language in texts was the first red flag and, soon after, my son broke up with her. It was sad to see such a sweet girl change so quickly. It was all manifested in texts.

By the way, I shouldn't have to remind you to never, *never* text and drive, right? You're acting like an irresponsible drunk driver in denial when you think you can look at your cell phone for even a second and not have it affect your driving.

So, what's an Instagram star supposed to do? When you're at a family event or with other human life forms, show some constraint. Acknowledge that the people in the room with you mean something to you. Connect with them. Talk to them. Be with them. You can always politely excuse yourself to use the restroom for five minutes and get your Facebook fix there. Join the world. Be a part of a flash mob or make a funny video with whatever song happens to be the cool thing at the moment. Don't just watch the world pass you by on your computer screen. Put your cell phone down, get out there, and live it.

Write down a list of all the fun things you can do *without* a cell phone:

*

*

*

*

*

*

Having a hard time thinking of things? Below are a few things you should do to rejoin society and learn some social skills:

* Learn how to play a musical instrument. You know you've been considering the guitar lately.
* Order for yourself at a restaurant. You're a big boy now; talk to humans.
* Talk to store clerks and cashiers. You're not invisible, and neither are they.
* Get a summer job. Learn how to deal with coworkers and customers.
* Put away your cell phone and play a board game.
* Have a conversation with an adult.
* Stand with good posture. People notice. Pull your shoulders back, for starters. Then imagine that a string is sewn to the middle of your chest and is gently pulling upward. Try that. How does that make you feel? Not convinced yet? Tuck in your tummy. There you go. You look *fabulous*! Two snaps!
* Look up when you cross the street rather than down at your cell phone. That one tip alone could save you from being run over by a car one day. I just saved your life. You're welcome.
* Realize that the entire world doesn't really care what you had for lunch today and they don't need to see a picture of it or read your commentary about it.
* Shave off your mullet. Join the real world.

Now, don't get me wrong. I'm not saying to throw away your cell phone. Just learn to control it before it controls you. A smart phone doesn't make you smart, but using it wisely can. There is a famous poem called the "Serenity Prayer" that I'm tweaking to be

God, grant me the serenity to reject the calls I should not take,
The courage to answer the ones I should,
And the wisdom to know the difference.

SECRET TIP ABOUT PARENTS

Now, you may hate this suggestion, but I promise that if you teach your parents how to use their own cell phones, they won't be as annoyed when they see you with yours. Here are some cool things you can show them how to do with their cell phones. They'll be totally impressed and think you're a genius:

* Program your TiVo or Roku.
* Shop for bargains using apps like Coupon Sherpa or NearbyNow.
* Listen to podcasts.
* Track calories and workouts, or use personal trainer apps.
* Get discounts by scanning QR codes or downloading coupons with Cellfire.
* Earn rewards when you're out painting the town with apps like We Reward.
* Trace your kids' locations.
* Catch your favorite TV show with MobiTV or MediaFLO.
* Stream your iTunes.
* Get RSS feeds with free services like Flurry or NetVibes2Go.
* Convert voicemail to text with apps like SimulScribe.
* Scan a document or business card with the free app Scanr.
* Leave notes for yourself on Evernote or Jott.
* Remote access your computer with Avvenu.

Here I am encouraging you to use your cell phone after telling you not to be addicted to it. Just use it as a tool, not a life. I'm assuming you have the scriptures and hymns on your cell phone, right? Here are some other cool LDS apps you can also share with your parents and use for yourself. Many of them are free!

* LDS Scripture Mastery Pro—Memorize those seminary scripture mastery verses finally!
* LDS Game Bundle

* LDS Pictures and Photos—Keep little ones quiet during sacrament meeting by looking at pretty LDS pictures.
* LDS Kids
* The Mormon Match Game
* LDS Hangman
* LDS Temples Quiz
* LDS Teens
* My Daily Book of Mormon Devotional
* LDS Quorum of the Twelve Apostles
* LDS Gospel Trivia

For all things physical, there is a spiritual equivalent. So, what's the spiritual equivalent of a cell phone? Prayer! Jesus has already paid the bill and will always answer. You'll never get a busy signal and you can talk as long as you want, without ever getting in trouble with your parents! Like a cell phone, don't do all of the talking—listen too.

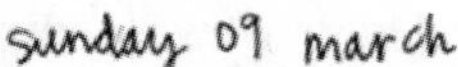

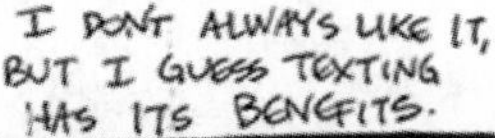

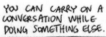

3-D Glasses

A movie hit the big screen in April 2014 entitled *God's Not Dead*. Before the movie ended, the lights turned on in the theater with a challenge for viewers to text people on their contact list the words "God's Not Dead." What a fantastic use of a cell phone! During the same week, I was watching a BYU–Idaho devotional on my computer and the speaker invited the students attending to send a text message of gratitude to someone they knew. Now we're talking! So much good can be accomplished with your cell phone!

FOR THE GUYS' EYES ONLY

Never break up with a girl over a text. *Never* "sext." *Never* take pictures you wouldn't want your mother to see. *Always* text kind words.

For the Lasses with Glasses

A guy may actually be trying to flirt with you by catching your eye. If you never look up from your cell phone, you might miss the love of your life! "Sexting" is *not* flirtatious fun; it is a red flag that the guy is a sleezeball and not a gentleman.

RANDOM JOKE ABOUT GLASSES

What did the cell phone that wore glasses say?

"I lost my contacts."

SUCCESS TIPS FROM MY WISE FRIENDS WHO KNOW HOW TO LIVE

- It's not about one man or woman doing a million things that will change the world, but millions of people doing what they can. —Deirdra Eden (She is the talented author of *The Watchers*. She also says, "No matter how dark the night, the sun will rise, and you will rise as well.")
- You'll remember everyone who has been either kind or cruel to you; others will also remember how you treated them. You'll never regret choosing kindness. —Annette Luthy Lyon (She is an award-winning author who serves as the "Grammar Nazi" in our LDS writers' group! Check out her website at www.AnnetteLyon.com.)
- I plan on arriving in heaven with skid-marks and telling God, "Wow! What a ride *that* was!" —Kevin Johnson

CHAPTER ELEVEN

Phantom of the Opera Mask: Developing Talents

Besides occasional youth service activities and helping guys with their Eagle Scout projects, this is the only time in your life when you really get to focus on yourself. Don't get me wrong. You *should* be doing lots of service for others your entire life. What I mean is that you generally aren't responsible for paying all of the bills and feeding and clothing other people. You may *want* to clothe someone, like your best friend who shows up at school looking like a complete dweeb, but that's a different chapter.

Now is the time in your life when you get to concentrate on developing your own talents, interests, and knowledge. Once you're married and have your own children, you'll need to take care of your family's needs first, before you run off to play tennis or take an art class at the community center. Until then, sign up for all of those classes! Try everything! Well, okay, not everything—just everything that is moral, legal, and non-fattening!

Don't laugh, but I've been trying to learn how to play the violin. If you heard me play, you *would* laugh. My youngest son plays the cello in his middle school orchestra. I was really tempted to ask his teacher if I could join the orchestra, but I knew that would make him a complete social outcast so I restrained myself. He absolutely hates practicing and acts like my husband and I are torturing him with wet noodles every time we remind him to put in the amount of practice hours that his teacher requires. He doesn't appreciate how lucky he is to get free lessons and be a part of a performing group. I never got to do that growing up. (I'm playing sad violin music for myself right now.)

The thing is that I would *love* to have enough time in the day so that I could practice playing the violin! I would *love* to have a musical talent, but I just don't have enough time in my busy day. (Not to mention that I don't have enough talent either.)

Your parents *want* you to discover and develop your talents. Some of your parents might even fantasize about seeing you on national TV with your amazing talent, thanking them in front of millions for encouraging you to practice when you were younger. Make them proud!

So, what are some things you want to learn how to do?

Answer these questions:

- What instrument would you like to learn how to play?
- What sport would you like to earn a scholarship for because you're so good at it?
- What topic would you like to learn more about?
- Have you ever written a poem?
- Do you know how to play pool?
- What can you draw?
- Can you make your pet do tricks?
- What sport are you the best at playing?
- How many pull-ups can you do?
- Have you ever tried ice-skating or roller-blading?
- Do you know how to ballroom dance?
- Can you speak a foreign language?
- Do you know how to design robots?
- Can you make creative mash-ups by combining different songs?
- Do you know how to do calligraphy with those fancy pens?
- Are you able to explain to an old person how to install new software on their computer and use it? (If so, please come to my house.)
- Can you choreograph a dance routine that gives people goose bumps when they watch it?
- Are you a cheerleader who can do splits when being thrown up in the air?
- Can you slam-dunk a basketball?

Start writing a list of some of the talents you would like to possess. They won't just come to you automatically. To achieve some level of excellence requires dedication, practice, and time. Of course, you don't have to be an expert at everything. Just pick one or two things you'd like to be really great at. Remember, you won't be awesome at everything you try. Welcome to the world of us mere mortals. Albert Einstein said, "Everybody is a genius. But if you judge a fish by its ability to climb a tree, it will live its whole life believing that it is stupid." We all know Einstein was a brainiac, but he wasn't very talented when it came to taming his mane. See, you can't be perfect at everything!

What are your talents right now?

*

*

*

*

*

If you plan on serving a mission, be sure to add these two to your list:

* Learn how to conduct music in 2/4, 3/4, and 6/8 time. Ask your ward chorister to show you how and she would be thrilled to teach you! Missionaries are often asked to lead the music in every single church meeting they attend. You might as well learn it now so you don't have to figure out what the old lady in your branch in Botswana is trying to say to you.
* Learn to play four songs on the piano for sacrament meeting. Every time I got transferred to a new area on my mission, the first question I was asked by the members there was, "Can you play the piano?" I felt like such a loser every time I had to mumble, "No." What's worse is that I had taken piano lessons when I was a little girl, but I didn't

remember a thing. Well, I could play "Chopsticks" still, but the members of the Church there weren't very impressed by that. Why four songs? You'll need an opening hymn, sacrament hymn, "rest" hymn in between talks, and then a closing hymn. It doesn't have to be fancy-schmancy with all of the chords; being able to play the melody is just fine. The members of the Church whom I served in Spain would have been thrilled if I could have simply played the basic notes. It would have helped them sing in tune too. I'm just saying.

Remember, not all talents are performance based. In other words, you don't have to sing and dance in order to have a valid talent. Ask yourself these questions to see if you already possess these skills or want to develop them:

- Can you inspire a group of people to accomplish a certain goal?
- Are you the "class clown" who can make people laugh?
- Do you know a bunch of trivia?
- Can you sense when people are feeling down and you know just what to say to make them feel better?
- Are you naturally thoughtful and it's easy for you to remember people's birthdays?
- Can you memorize things really easily?
- Do you have an entrepreneurial spirit that has allowed you to create your own money-making business?
- Is it easy for you to brainstorm because you have so many creative ideas?

The point of developing all of these skills and talents isn't a contest to see who has the most by the time we die. There are several purposes:

- Use them to help build the kingdom of God on earth.
- Enrich your life with wondrous variety.

Did you know you can ask Heavenly Father to bless you with special gifts of the Spirit? He will bless you with more abilities for your own benefit, as well as to use them in blessing others. Some of the gifts include speaking a foreign language and healing others, and receiving wisdom, faith, knowledge, and Christlike love. For a description of the gifts of the Spirit, study Doctrine and Covenants 46:11–33; 1 Corinthians 12:1–12; and Moroni 10:8–18.

I had a really unusual experience in college that taught me how eager the Lord is to bless us with spiritual gifts. I was on the Speech and Debate team at BYU and had just returned to the house where I was living after a weekend away at a tournament. My boyfriend was waiting for me at the door with a concerned look on his face, and I knew that something was wrong. Just then, one of my roommates ran out of the door crying. What was going on?

My boyfriend carried in my suitcase for me (score Gentleman Points!) and then he explained that my roommate had practically thrown herself at him all weekend while I was out of town. He assured me that he was not interested in her but wanted me to forgive her and not be angry. What the . . . ? I *was* angry and felt betrayed by my very own roommate. He told me how lonely she was and how I should be understanding about her aggressive search for romance. #ExcuseMe?

I was furious with her and, to be honest, even a little suspicious of my boyfriend for possibly leading her on. I knew I was going to have to deal with her eventually because we lived in the same house, so I walked upstairs to my bedroom and immediately fell to my knees next to my bed to pray for the Lord's guidance on this one.

I whined and complained to God for a few minutes, but then when I sincerely asked for an understanding heart, the love poured into me. In fact, I was so overwhelmed with love for this girl who had tried to steal my boyfriend that I was surprised at how easy it was for me to feel forgiveness toward her. I was completely washed over with a Christlike love for both of them, and I'll never forget the power of that moment. Later, I spoke with each of them, and I remember how odd it was that I was so calm and kind. I knew that outpouring of unconditional love didn't come from me.

The strength of that gift comes and goes in my life, but now I know that it is there any time I need extra help. When the Lord promises us help or blessings, He really does keep His word. We study the scriptures in church, seminary, and even in family home evening, but that time is wasted if we're not *applying* what we learn to our lives.

"Good music is one of the greatest tools we have for getting the gospel inside of us," wrote the talented Janice Kapp Perry in a recent Facebook message to me. I had asked her to share some advice for you about how to develop talents, achieve success, and be happy in this life. She replied, "Keep an uplifting song in your heart at all times!" Now, I have a terrible singing voice, but even I can make a song sound beautiful in my heart!

Phantom of the Opera Mask

By the way, you should definitely recognize Janice Kapp Perry's name! She has written a *ton* of LDS music that we sing at church all of the time. Isn't that cool that she sent me something to share with you in this book? She is so talented, but did you know that she didn't even begin writing songs until later in life? Just because you don't think you have any talents now doesn't mean that they won't reveal themselves later!

Janice Kapp Perry's big goal was to sing in the Mormon Tabernacle Choir, but she admits that she doesn't have a great voice and knew she would never be allowed in to the world-famous choir. After writing hundreds of beautiful songs, the choir invited her to join them and said, "Sometimes we make exceptions." Isn't that awesome? She has such a great sense of humor and never gave up on her dreams. You can learn more about her beautiful spirit and music at www.janicekappperry.com. She is a terrific example of how to work hard at developing a talent and then use it to enrich the lives of others.

Another great musician who inspires me is Steven Sharp Nelson. You know him best as the cellist in the popular group The Piano Guys. He has such a great sense of humor and passion that are visible in his YouTube videos. When I asked him to share some success advice for all of you, he had quite a bit to say! He said,

> The best advice I've ever received was from President Ezra Taft Benson: "Men and women who turn their lives over to God will discover that He can make a lot more out of their lives than they can. He can deepen their joys, expand their vision, quicken their minds, strengthen their muscles, lift their spirits, multiply their blessings, increase their opportunities, comfort their souls, and pour out peace." When I follow this advice, happiness and success come naturally.

But wait! There's more! Steven also said,

> Don't take yourself too seriously. Get over yourself. Laugh *with* yourself when you make mistakes. Cut yourself some slack. The man at ease with himself is at ease with others, and with the world. Take Helaman's advice (Alma 37): Pray over *everything*—for *all* thy support. Don't save your prayers for the "big stuff." The little stuff *is* the big stuff. Pray that you'll know what to study most for your test. Pray when you're talking to a friend that you can help her know how loved by God she is. Pray that your "bad hair day" will turn around. And when He answers your prayer, say a prayer of thanks.

Of course, Steven's musical talents are such a big part of his life that he wanted to share his thoughts with you on the importance of choosing good music. He said,

> The music you listen to is your life's soundtrack. It will shape your mood, your ambitions, and most importantly, it will either invite or deny the Spirit's presence in your life. If you hear a bad lyric, change the channel. If you're in a place with bad music, leave. Make a playlist of inspiring, motivating songs that get you to feel the Spirit and when you've hit a rough patch, put on headphones, close your eyes, and hit play. The adversary has so little power over people who constantly surround themselves with a soundtrack of good music.

Great advice, right? I couldn't have said it better. (I didn't.) Take a look at Steven's website at www.StevenSharpNelson.com. You can also subscribe to The Piano Guys on their YouTube or Pandora channels or check them out at thepianoguys.com.

Phantom of the Opera Mask

Finally, **write down your three biggest failures and your three biggest successes**. Next to each of them, **write down some of the events that lead up to the positive or negative results**. Look for patterns, without regret or pride, that will teach you about how you used each experience to drive you forward.

Successes:

1.

2.

3.

Lessons learned:

*

*

Epic Fails:

1.

2.

3.

Lessons learned:

*

*

What are your strengths?

*

*

*

What are your weaknesses?

*

*

*

FOR THE GUYS' EYES ONLY

I asked my husband what advice he had for you guys on developing talents. He said that if you understand the concept of compound interest, then you should know that it also works the same with talents. For example, if you start saving ten percent of your income now, you'll be a millionaire by the time you're thirty. Work on developing talents *early* in your life and you'll be great by the time you're his age. #OldGeezerHusband

He always says how he wishes he could go back to his teenage years and use his time more wisely. He admits that he wasted a *lot* of time doing nothing. He regrets that he doesn't have anything to show for all of that time. He said he spent way too much time trying to be cool. Try instead to be talented!

Video games are fun, but they shouldn't be your life. This is the part where I tell you to cut down the amount of time you spend playing video games. Blah blah blah blabla blah. Yeah, I know that's what you hear when parents start to lecture about gaming. The truth is that video games suck hours out of your day and life. I know. I have four sons, remember? And, yeah, I know girls play too. Sure, you learn eye-hand coordination skills that will come in handy if you become a drone operator in the military, but you need to make sure you know how to fill your spare time with other activities that will develop meaningful talents and qualities. Whenever I turn off video games at my house, my kids will sometimes sit in a stupor, not knowing what to do with themselves. That's not good.

The Word of Wisdom teaches us the importance of "moderation in all things." That applies to gaming. What you're ingesting into your body for hours at a time when you play video games is usually violence. Set a timer and then, when it goes off, stop playing and move on to a different activity that helps you become the man you truly want to become.

I totally "get" that a guy has to have playtime with his "bros." Once you're married, you need to arrange for "broments," as well as encourage your wife to set aside time for "Girls Night Out." It's healthy for both of you. What will hurt your marriage is if you haven't learned how to manage your time or be disciplined enough to step away from the video games when the dishes need to be done. Yeah, that's right. You heard me. You *will* be doing dishes.

Girls are suckers for modern-day stripling warriors. Check out all of their qualities in Alma 53 and work on adding them to your list of strengths:

- Exceedingly valiant for courage, strength, and activity.
- Men true at all times in whatsoever thing they were entrusted.
- Men of truth and soberness.
- Keep the commandments of God.
- Walk uprightly before God.

For the Lasses with Glasses

Women have historically been the ones who are expected to bring refinement and culture to society. Your talents are what will soften a home and convert it from a wild bachelor pad into a nurturing refuge for your family.

Talents that will come in handy when raising your children include party planning, home management, organization, scrapbooking, sewing, memorizing, budgeting, and so much more. You will wear many hats as a wife and mother. Anyone who has ever said that multitasking makes you less focused has never been a mother. Learn to keep lists and charts and checklists.

Phantom of the Opera Mask

Do you remember the part in the Book of Mormon that talks about the valiant stripling warriors and how they praised their mothers for having such strong faith? They attributed their success in battle to the teachings of their mothers. What a wonderful tribute. Add to your list of talents: scriptorian. Some girls marry returned missionaries, thinking that they will be the gospel expert in the family. Yes, we honor their priesthood leadership, but don't take a backseat to the spiritual nurturing of your children.

By the way, have you ever wondered where the dads of the stripling warriors were during that time? They were actually away from the village getting provisions. It was a time of war and the men had been called away to get provisions (Alma 56:27). What would you do if your husband had to leave you and your children for a time and you were left alone to take care of everything at home? Do you know how to change an air filter? Can you rewire a broken toaster? Can you change a flat tire? Do you know when to plant seeds for a summer vegetable garden? Develop some of those skills so that you can be capable of running a household with or without a man.

RANDOM JOKE ABOUT GLASSES

What happened to the lab tech when he fell into the lens grinder?
—He made a spectacle of himself

SUCCESS TIPS FROM MY TALENTED FRIENDS

- Love yourself. —Leslie Gansel Bauscher
- Never give up on your dreams; you never know when just a little more effort and hard work will be what it takes to get you there! Perfect is the enemy of good. —Jonathan Kaplan
- You have gifts that are only yours. Discover them, develop them, and share them as often as you can. —Jordan Bluth (He is a super humble guy with a fantastic voice. Check him out at www.JordanBluth.com.)
- The best way to strengthen your talents is to use them to serve others. Remember, that is why you have them in the first place. —Michael Young (He sings in the Mormon Tabernacle Choir! His Facebook profile picture shows him holding the recent Grammy Award the choir won! In the premortal world I stood in line to get a good singing voice. Then the Relief Society sisters brought out the ice cream and I switched lines. True story.)

CHAPTER TWELVE

Ski Goggles: Seeing Things the Mirror Doesn't Show You

You only get one. "One what?" you ask. You only get one chance to make a first impression? One chance to find your soul mate? One chance to win the lottery? One pair of ski goggles? (What's up with the ski goggles?) No, something much more significant. You only get one body.

In this society of quick fixes and throw-away purchases, it's easy to replace almost anything. Even with the amazing medical technologies and advances of plastic surgery that allow us to replace certain body parts (have you seen most of the celebrities lately?), you still only get one body. The good news is that it comes with a lifetime warranty, although the quality is not guaranteed. That is up to you. How you treat it carries the marks of abuse, misuse, or respect.

As you gain more understanding of your "tabernacle of clay" (Moroni 9:6), you may gain a deeper appreciation for your body, a greater respect for its abilities and limitations, a profound reverence for the Divine Architect, and a more peaceful love for yourself and others around you.

They say happiness is having your health. If that's true, then what are you *doing* about it? Heavenly Father is such a loving God because not only does he give us spiritual laws to help us know how to return to live with him, but he also gives us physical laws for the same purpose.

Ski Goggles

The Word of Wisdom was given to us to protect us from harm. You know how Heavenly Father feels about temples, don't you? They are sacred and holy. Your body is sacred and holy too! In 1 Corinthians 3:17, the Lord compares your body to a temple. A vessel is a container that holds something. Your physical body is the vessel that holds your spirit.

There is a very close relationship between physical health and your spiritual development. When you neglect or abuse your body, you are less sensitive to the Spirit. When you drink alcohol, smoke any substance, or do drugs, you're handing over your moral agency to things that control your mind. They will dull your conscience until you can't hear the "still, small voice" of the Spirit. One of the biggest tests of coming to earth was to see if we could handle a body. I'm sure we confidently said, "Sure, no problema, hombre." Now that we're here, it's not so easy, is it? I mean, they keep inventing amazing things I want to eat that will clog my arteries and make me fat!

When I was first trained to teach water aerobics at a fitness center, my instructor would always say, "Movement is the celebration of life!" I thought that was such an empowering thought that made me want to move! Then, he would quietly warn, "Pain is the reminder that we're alive." Ha ha.

I work with a *lot* of students in college who do drugs and smoke marijuana. (Not my sweet BYU–I students!) They love to debate all the reasons why marijuana should be legal in every state. They're idiots. Can I speak any plainer than that? Sure, your friends may try to persuade you to partake, using seemingly clever arguments. If they do, they're idiots too. The Creator of the entire universe and beyond has told us not to put those things in our bodies. I think He knows better than your doped-out friends.

Recently, I was teaching a night class when two of my students showed up higher than a kite, if you know what I mean. One of them could barely walk and the other one could hardly keep his eyes open. A week earlier, they had both chimed in during a class discussion about how smoking marijuana actually helped them be better drivers. They couldn't even function in class. A couple of real geniuses. They were the best visual aid I could have asked for to illustrate how marijuana impairs your cognitive abilities. That's a fancy way of saying, "Drugs make you stupid."

Ski Goggles

You've heard the phrase "cleanliness is next to godliness." Right? Here's a little self-evaluation health quiz to see if there are some areas where you can take better care of your precious temple. Circle **YES** or **NO.**

- I bathe at least every other day and change into clean clothes.
  YES **NO**
- I brush my teeth twice a day.
  YES **NO**
- I have had up-to-date vaccinations.
  YES **NO**
- I wash my hands often and always before eating.
  YES **NO**
- I retire to bed early.
  YES **NO**
- I arise early.
  YES **NO**
- I sleep at least six to eight hours each night.
  YES **NO**
- I engage in strenuous physical activity at least three times a week.
  YES **NO**
- I try to arrange my time so that I walk more than I ride or sit.
  YES **NO**
- I am careful about how much candy and soda I consume.
  YES **NO**
- I drink six to eight glasses of water each day.
  YES **NO**
- I abstain from alcohol, tobacco, tea, coffee, and harmful drugs.
  YES **NO**
- I obey the Word of Wisdom.
  YES **NO**
- I eat five servings of fruits and vegetables a day.
  YES **NO**

From the very beginning, our Father in Heaven has demonstrated His concern for our physical well-being. It is written that the Lord "doeth not anything save it be for the benefit of the world" (2 Nephi 26:24). The Lord created us, so He definitely knows what will help or hurt us. The Lord directed Adam in the proper use of herbs and crops of the field (Genesis 1:29–30). Later he instructed Noah in the use of meat and herbs (Genesis 9:3).

To the children of Israel under Moses, the Lord gave some detailed dietary instructions and said, "For thou art an holy people unto the Lord thy God, and the Lord hath chosen thee to be a peculiar people unto himself, above all the nations that are upon the earth. Thou shalt not eat any abominable thing" (Deuteronomy 14:2-3). In New Testament times, the Lord instructed His people not to be given to wine (1 Timothy 3:3).

In this dispensation, the Lord gave the Word of Wisdom (D&C 89) to help us be strong and healthy. He expects us to use wise judgment based upon these principles.

Ski Goggles

When I was a little girl, I had a Primary teacher explain to me that I only had to decide once in my life whether I would smoke or drink alcohol. I only had to choose one time whether I wanted the words "smoker" or "drinker" to describe me. That made sense to me. Once I decided not to partake of such harmful substances I wouldn't have to think about it ever again. My teacher handed each one of us a card upon which we could write our commitments to ourselves about living the Word of Wisdom. I still have that card and have been true to my promise ever since then!

Keeping the Word of Wisdom is really a no-brainer. I mean, everyone knows smoking is harmful. So don't smoke. Easy. We know that taking drugs and drinking alcohol is bad for our bodies too. So don't use them. You *know* this. The temptation occurs when someone cool asks you to do it. You are *way* cooler if you don't. Trust me. You're going to let some zit-faced kid who won't even remember you in five years determine your obedience, worthiness, and health? Lame. There are worse things than not being cool in front of that kid. You'll be a bishop some day, while that dumb kid will be wearing a wife-beater T-shirt and drinking a beer on his front lawn. (Peace out! Trina lets the microphone drop to the floor.)

President Spencer W. Kimball and his wife were touring in Europe in 1937 and attended a very fancy banquet in a fashionable hotel. The many waiters moved about the tables, which were decorated with beautiful silver, linen, fancy serving dishes, and seven wine glasses. President Kimball said that the temptation nudged him: "Shall I drink it or at least sip it? No one who cares will know." He said it was quite a temptation, but then the thought came to him that he had made a firm resolution as a boy that he would never touch the forbidden things. He had already lived a third of a century firm and resolute so he would not break his record. He counseled, "Now is the time to set your life's goals. Now is the time to set your standards firmly and then hold to them throughout your life." He didn't touch a drop. No one seemed to notice if he did or didn't, except the Lord and himself. ("President Kimball Speaks Out on Planning Your Life," *New Era*, Sept. 1981)

Ski Goggles

The comedian A. Whitney Brown said, "I am not a vegetarian because I love animals; I am a vegetarian because I hate plants." (Little joke there.) The Word of Wisdom isn't just about what *not* to eat or drink. It also contains counsel on the things we need to *do* to maintain good health. Like exercising and wearing those ski goggles while you do sports! (I'll bet you were wondering if I'd ever get around to explaining that picture at the top of the chapter.)

If you need a little extra help with your health, try these vitamins:

- Vitamin **A—"A**ll things work together for good to them that love God" (Romans 8:28).
- Vitamin **B—"B**e still, and know that I am God" (Psalms 46:10).
- Vitamin **C—"C**asting all your care upon him; for he careth for you" (1 Peter 5:7).
- Vitamin **D—"D**raw near to God" (Psalms 73:28).

FOR THE GUYS' EYES ONLY

Young men, you are to do the Lord's work and labor in building the kingdom—real, physical things like passing the sacrament, healing the sick, knocking on doors for hours on your mission, and carrying boxes to help the new family in the ward move in. You need to get in shape and build those muscles.

I knew a remarkable woman who only had about twenty-eight percent heart capacity and struggled for years until her heart finally didn't have the strength any more. She told me that once when she was in the hospital after losing her ability to control her body, she thought to herself that she had finally lost her agency. She understood that our bodies are truly gifts from our Father in Heaven that enable us to learn to be like him.

Learn to curb your physical passions. The feelings you have are natural and put inside you by a loving God who wants you to be attracted to girls. The feelings aren't bad, just don't act on them . . . yet. You'll have plenty of time to act on them when you're married. Learn how to control your desires and you will conquer your body.

I'm sure you've heard a million talks about the dangers of pornography by now. Everything you've heard is true. It is vile and will turn your God-given desires into something ugly. Don't go there. Don't. Don't. Don't.

Do you hear me? (Is this thing on? Trina taps on the microphone.) Don't. Don't. Don't.

Several years ago, my son's priesthood leaders put those big paperclip clamps on all of the boys' scriptures. They wondered why he was being so weird until he explained the acronym:

- C = Commitment to the commandments.
- L = Listen and learn from the Spirit.
- A = Act like the priesthood holder you are.
- M = Mission preparation begins today.
- P = Pray until you get an answer.
- S = Study the scriptures instead of just read them.

Put clamps on everything to remind you to prepare your body and spirit every day to be used by the Lord to do His work!

For the Lasses with Glasses

In a society that values Botox more than health, it is no surprise that increasing depression rates and plummeting self-image are the results. As a mother, Young Women president, seminary teacher, and college professor, I have seen thousands of youth who question and doubt the inherent beauty of their body and personal value. Too much emphasis is placed on what the mirror tells us about physical beauty and how our value in society is determined by that judgment. Do you judge your beauty and personal worth by your reflection from a piece of glass? You realize it doesn't tell the whole story of you, right?

God created many wonderful things: plants, animals, fish, foul, flowers, and trees. *Then* He created you. He didn't just say you were His finest creation; He said you were *family*.

Young women, because you are to be a co-creator with God, He needs to use you as His instrument in a very *physical* way: to have babies, serve others, clean someone's house when they're sick, and take meals to people. You need to be careful with that sacred power of carrying and giving life. It is a true miracle.

Be gentle with your bodies and learn to listen to them. They will tell you when something is wrong. What you put into your body is reflected on what's on the outside of your body. Eat healthy, exercise, sweat, inhale deeply, drink lots of water. Good girl!

Ski Goggles

Exercise can help beat depression. It can be especially important for girls who suffer with PMS. Girls are two times more likely than men to suffer from depression. Great, yet one more reason to be depressed! Depression can be caused by a chemical imbalance in your body, fluctuating hormones, or stupid Satan trying to make you less effective so that you aren't a force for good in the world.

If you're feeling low, remember that the sun has a sinking spell every night, but it keeps coming back up every morning!

RANDOM JOKE ABOUT GLASSES

Nick goes into the optometrist's office. He opens the door and says to the receptionist, "I think I need my eyes checked." She says, "You're not kidding. This is the Ladies' Room."

SUCCESS TIPS FROM MY WISE FRIENDS WHO WANT YOU TO BE HAPPY

- God gives us the strength to follow our dreams, achieve the impossible and embrace the limitless opportunities for the future! —Natalee Lence (She writes beautiful instrumental music and has a new album coming out. She's a devoted mother of four and wanted me to tell you how important you are in the Lord's eyes. Check out her talents at www.NataleeLence.com.)
- Stay away from drugs! Name one good thing that comes from doing drugs. You can't, can you? Then why bother? The only things it brings are destruction of your brain, enslavement of your body, family and marital problems, financial problems, job difficulties, and crime. There are no redeeming qualities from doing them. They are a tool of Satan. Your body is a sacred gift of God. Don't throw it away by abusing it. No one ever grew up saying they wanted to be a druggie. No drug addict ever thought that it would lead them to a life of misery. —Paula Flatman
- Do you think your nose is too big? Your ears are funny looking? Who cares? If someone judges you by those kinds of things, they're really not interested in what's in your heart and, therefore, not worth having as friends anyway. —Sean Flemming

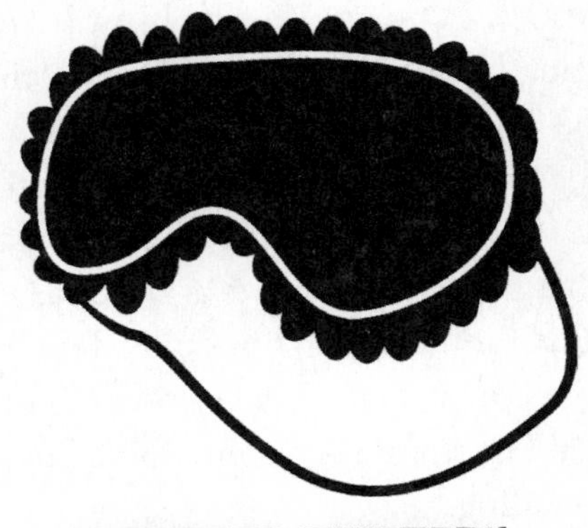

CHAPTER THIRTEEN

Sleeping Mask: Enlightened Darkness

I remember walking into my parents' bedroom in the wee hours of the night when I was a little girl and seeing my mother wear one of those weird sleeping masks over her eyes. Aren't those just for old people and movie stars? Well, I'm definitely not a movie star (although I was a movie extra once on a TV series that never aired!) and I'm not *that* old yet, but I get it now. When you're exhausted and know you *have* to get some sleep because you have a big "thing" the next morning, you're actually willing to wear one of those silly masks so that it's dark and nothing will wake you up. Okay, maybe I *am* getting that old.

When you're young, you can live on a Snickers bar and iTune fumes, but that doesn't mean you should. When I was your age, I thought I could conquer the world. Now I just want a nap. I never thought I'd actually get old and feel crummy all the time. I used to look at cranky old people and wonder why they had to be so mean. Now I understand that it's mostly because they just don't feel well! (A few of them actually *are* mean on purpose.) Think about how unpleasant you can be when you're sick or tired. C'mon, admit it.

I learned that simple lesson when I was on bed rest during a difficult pregnancy with my fourth son. My body was really struggling so my doctor told me to not move or else I might lose the baby. It's pretty amazing what women will do to bring life into this world. (Be sure to thank your mom.) I felt crummy all the time and you could say I was not exactly the most cheerful person to be around. I had a new appreciation for people with chronic diseases who would never recover. I knew at least that if I followed my doctor's orders that I would get a prize at the end: a healthy baby boy. I gained greater empathy for those who hurt and whose pain won't end until they're released from this mortal life. It was a sobering lesson and one that I try to remember when I'm around someone who is cranky and requires my patience and understanding.

So, back to the sleep mask and sleep topic. You need to get some sleep, my young friend. I know you want to stay up super late and play, but you know you'll be tired and less than pleasant the next day. You know I'm right. You know your parents are right when they tell you, "Go to bed *now*!" They want you to be your best self the next day.

Even more important is the fact that the Holy Ghost goes to bed at midnight. Did you know that? It's true. You simply can't make good decisions after midnight. Some of the worst ideas are thought up when you're out late with friends and getting silly. How do I know that? Because I was once a teenager too. I've also raised four of them.

Do I want you to be silly and have fun with your friends? Absolutely! Make terrific memories! I even forced my boys and their friends to go toilet paper the bishop's house. Of course, I made them return the next day to help clean up the mess too. (Aren't I a great mom?) Just know that lack of sleep and brilliant ideas don't go together. Quite a few studies have been done that show a sleep-deprived driver is as dangerous as a drunk driver. Let that sentence sink in.

Before I go on, I need to give you a standing ovation for being so awesome. (This is me standing up, clapping, and cheering. I'm also doing that loud whistle with my two fingers in my mouth.) If you're in high school, then you're going to seminary and carrying a heavy load of classes on top of all of your other activities. If you're going to early-morning seminary, then you're a total rock star. I'm so proud of you. Every other teenager out there is catching *zs* while you're studying scriptures!

This section of the poem "The Ladder of St. Augustine" by Henry Wadsworth Longfellow describes *you* perfectly:

> The heights by great men reached and kept
> Were not attained by sudden flight,
> But they, while their companions slept,
> Were toiling upward in the night.

A friend of mine asked her kids what they thought she should write above their front door to remind them to make good choices when leaving the house. You know we Mormon moms love to put those vinyl letters all over everything lately. She figured her kids would suggest something like "Return With Honor" or "Choose the Right" or an inspiring verse from the scriptures. A few days later, one of her kids came to her and said excitedly, "I know what I want above our door! It should be something that you always remind us every time we walk out the door!" She tried to think of what it could possibly be and laughed when he proclaimed, "Don't do anything stupid!" Yep, that's what's over her front door now!

What's interesting is that inspiration often comes in the morning light and rarely in the dark of night. Elder Richard G. Scott gave a great talk about how to receive personal revelation in the spring general conference of 2012. He said,

> Spiritual communication can be enhanced by good health practices. Exercise, reasonable amounts of sleep, and good eating habits increase our capacity to receive and understand revelation. . . . Revelation can also be given in a dream when there is an almost imperceptible transition from sleep to wakefulness. If you strive to capture the content immediately, you can record great detail. ("How to Obtain Revelation and Inspiration for Your Personal Life," *Ensign*, May 2012)

Keep an inspiration journal by your bed. The Lord will often give you important information right after you pray at night and again in the morning. When you stay out late and are too tired to do anything more than roll inside your sheets without talking to Heavenly Father, you're missing a great opportunity to receive specific direction in your life.

Do you dream in color? Do you remember your dreams? One of my sons keeps a dream journal by his bed and records his impressions as soon as he wakes up. If you dream a lot, like he does, you might consider keeping one too. Certain patterns in your dreams could help you understand yourself better.

Do a keyword search in the scriptures at lds.org for the word "dream" and you find pages of references for when the Lord has spoken to His people through dreams. We know that form of communication will increase as we get closer the Savior's Second Coming: "And it shall come to pass in the last days, saith God, I will pour out of my Spirit upon all flesh: and your sons and your daughters shall prophesy, and your young men shall see visions, and your old men shall dream dreams" (Acts 2:17).

Now, that doesn't mean everything you dream means something significant. An avocado on a cat's head may just be a guacamole ingredient on a feline. There are tons of books out there that can help you analyze your dreams. When you try to figure out what your dreams mean, ask yourself some of these questions:

* Is the Lord trying to teach me something?
* Is my body trying to tell me something?
* Does the dream reveal a direction my life is going?
* Is this an answer to a question I have or problem I need to solve?

Sleeping Mask

Hey, did I mention that getting the correct amount of sleep is actually a commandment? It is! Read Doctrine and Covenants 88:124. Like all commandments, there is a promise associated with our loving obedience: "cease to sleep longer than is needful; retire to thy bed early, that ye may not be weary; arise early, that your bodies and your minds may be invigorated."

The truth is that spirituality and health go together. That's what the Word of Wisdom is supposed to teach us. The health guidelines are to help us keep our bodies, our personal temples, a place where the Spirit can dwell, but it won't if we don't take care of ourselves.

It's much harder to say meaningful prayers or get anything out of your scripture study when it's one o'clock in the morning, and one eye is closed and the other one is starting to droop. I'll never forget one wintery night in college when I stayed out *really* late with my friends. It was freezing inside my apartment when I got home, so I told Heavenly Father that I would kneel on top of my bed with my blankets over me for my evening prayer. I was cold and exhausted, and before I knew it, I had drifted to sleep right in the middle of a sentence during my prayer. Yeah, I'm sure Father was really impressed with me.

Some time later, who knows how much later, I woke up still in that same kneeling position I had started in under my covers. My legs were cramping and I thought I might be frozen in that position for the rest of my life. You know that feeling when the blood rushes back into your foot after it falls asleep and the tingling that hurts so much? It was like that, but a million times more painful. I immediately started praying again, this time promising the Lord that I would never do that again. Did I keep my promise? Nope. He knows that if I pray in bed late at night that He is free to walk out of my bedroom as soon as I start praying, because I'll be passed out in about thirteen seconds. Am I lame? Yep.

I'm so grateful for a loving Heavenly Father who is patient and forgiving. He probably just chuckles and rolls His eyes. I'm still trying to be better at going to bed on time and staying awake during my scripture study and prayers. Develop those good habits *now*, when you're young, so you won't have to spend your entire life trying to discipline yourself. Now, I'm going to take a nap.

FOR THE GUYS' EYES ONLY

If I told you that you'd grow taller if you got more sleep, would you go to bed on time from now on? Science tells us that your body grows and regenerates tissue while you're at rest. Go to bed!

Now, there are those of you out there who should be told the complete opposite advice: wake up! I have kids who sleep and sleep and sleep and *zzz . . . wake up*! You're missing life! Have you ever slept so long that you're actually tired when you wake up? Find the right balance that your body needs. How do you do that? Experiment and keep a record. Use something like this:

- **Monday**
  Hours of sleep I got last night:
  How I felt when I got up:
- **Tuesday**
  Hours of sleep I got last night:
  How I felt when I got up:
- **Wednesday**
  Hours of sleep I got last night:
  How I felt when I got up:
- **Thursday**
  Hours of sleep I got last night:
  How I felt when I got up:
- **Friday**
  Hours of sleep I got last night:
  How I felt when I got up:
- **Saturday**
  Hours of sleep I got last night:
  How I felt when I got up:
- **Sunday**
  Hours of sleep I got last night:
  How I felt when I got up:

Recognize that everyone requires a different amount of sleep. My husband can run circles around me on very few hours of sleep every night. When we first got married, he said he was going to wake up at three o'clock every morning to get a jump-start on the day, and would keep doing that until we were millionaires. Sadly, he's still waking up at three o'clock every day.

I have a sister who requires more hours of sleep than the average person. She's a hard worker and very productive when she's awake, but she needs to sleep! No judgment.

For the Lasses with Glasses

Be gentle with your bodies. I think I said that in the last chapter, because it's so important! Listen to your body. Fluctuating hormones can make you get depressed and want to sleep. Try not to sleep more than you need to. Sometimes you just need to take a walk around the block instead. You'll feel more invigorated and alive.

Take a peek at the tips I gave the guys. (I know you've been reading their sections all along anyway.) Track the number of hours you sleep and how you feel afterward in order to figure out what the right amount is for your body.

RANDOM JOKE ABOUT GLASSES

A patient who doesn't want to wear glasses anymore says to the optometrist, "I'm very worried about the outcome of this operation, Doctor. What are the chances?"

The optometrist says to the patient, "Don't worry. You won't be able to see the difference."

SUCCESS TIPS FROM MY WISE FRIENDS WHO ARE PROBABLY ASLEEP RIGHT NOW

- Who you believe you are is more important than what others believe. If you knew what God thinks of you, you could move mountains. —Lori Jones
- Choose confidence. It's a muscle and can become stronger the more you choose to exercise it. Confidence is your foundation for happiness. —Jessie Funk (Have you discovered her beautiful songs yet? She also founded Ivy Girl Academy, a nonprofit organization that empowers young women. Check out her YouTube channel and www.jessiefunk.com. With the last name of "Funk," you *know* she's awesome!)
- Drink more water than you think you need. Don't eat anything that's growing green fuzz on it. Stretch when you wake up. Go to bed with gratitude in your heart. That pretty much covers it. —Steven Kendrick

CHAPTER FOURTEEN

Rose-Colored Glasses: "The Grass Is Always Greener" Syndrome

Your future is so bright! You have so many exciting things to look forward to! Did you know that your happiness is intertwined with your outlook on life? It's easy to get caught in the trap of "I'll be happy . . .

. . . when I have a boyfriend."

. . . if I had different parents."

. . . if I didn't live in this town."

. . . when I have a different math teacher."

. . . if I could make the basketball team."

. . . when I can quit this job."

If and *when* sometimes never come. And if they do, it may not be as good as you had imagined. Perfection is a very tricky thing to wait for.

The expression "seeing through rose-colored glasses" means that someone sees an idealistic view of the world and not how things really are. An example is when you see a popular kid at school wearing a pair of awesome shoes and you wish you could have them too. You just know that your coolness factor will jump up several levels, and you must own them to improve your social standing and degree of happiness. Your parents warn that they cost too much money. But you know you're right; you'll show *them*! You work hard; save your money; and fantasize for weeks about how "dope" it'll be to walk into school with those incredible shoes on your feet, causing everyone to turn in slow motion and triumphantly chant your name in splendid glory. Then, when you can finally afford them and bring them home to wear, you realize they squish your big toe and give you a blister.

People who wish something were different in their lives so they can be truly happy often find that once that thing finally does happen, they're still not happy. Why is that? Because happiness is a state of mind. Happiness is something that happens inside of you, not outside. Abraham Lincoln once said, "Folks are about as happy as they make up their minds to be" (*Quote Investigator*). He sure had a lot of brains underneath that tall, black hat of his. Hmm . . . maybe that's why that hat was so tall.

While preparing for the future, appreciate the time of life you're in right now. Before you know it, today will be gone and you'll find that you spent your life wishing it away. Someone once said, "Today is God's gift to you;

that's why they call it the present." Besides, you need to have a rotten math teacher to create some horror stories to tell your own kids so they'll see how much you suffered. Right? Happiness is being grateful for what you *do* have. Stop focusing on what you don't.

Present Tense
Jason Lehman

It was spring, but it was summer I wanted:
The warm days, the great outdoors.
It was summer, but it was fall I wanted:
The colorful leaves, the cold, dry air.
It was fall, but it was winter I wanted:
The beautiful snow, the joy of the holiday season.
It was winter, but it was spring I wanted:
The warmth, the blossoming of nature.

I was a child, but it was adulthood I wanted:
The freedom, the respect.
I was twenty, but it was thirty I wanted:
To be mature and sophisticated.
I was single, but it was marriage I wanted:
The love, the companionship.
I was married, but it was single I wanted:
To be without responsibility or entanglements.
I was middle-aged, but it was twenty I wanted:
The presence of mind without limitations.
My life was over.
I never got what I wanted.

This next quote is so wise that it has been attributed to several different writers and posted in a hundred different styles on Pinterest, on T-shirts, and on bumper stickers: "Life isn't measured by the number of breaths we take, but by the moments that take our breath away." I love that! Stop and smell the roses! Life isn't a destination but a journey. Enjoy the trip!

Today feels like forever when you have a giant zit on your nose. Learn to laugh at all the dumb things in your life that really won't matter down the road. Comedy is tragedy plus time. Weird, right? It's true. You better start learning to laugh at yourself because you're not going to get out of this live alive (wink). Some day you *will* laugh at making an idiot of yourself in front of that super cute guy at school. In thirty years, he'll be married to a lady who weighs over four hundred pounds, and you'll be married to an even cuter guy who loves that you are silly and make him laugh. Embrace the klutzy geek inside of you. Life is messy and wonderful.

President Gordon B. Hinckley wisely quoted Jenkins Lloyd Jones when he pointed out, "Anyone who imagines that bliss is normal is going to waste a lot of time running around shouting that he has been robbed. [The fact is] most putts don't drop. Most beef is tough. Most children grow up to be just people. Most successful marriages require a high degree of mutual toleration. Most jobs are more often dull than otherwise. . . . The trick is to thank the Lord for letting you have the ride" ("A Conversation with Single Adults," *Ensign*, Mar. 1997).

I hope that doesn't depress you. The reality is that not all of us are going to be billionaires with perfect bodies and amazing lives. It's the expectations that often set us up for disappointment. (Those romance novels don't help.) Yes, of course reach for high goals! Absolutely set high standards! Just don't be shocked when your knight in shining armor shows up on a pony instead. If you're flexible and have an attitude of gratitude, you'll enjoy life's little twists rather than be constantly annoyed and frustrated by them.

As studies in perception indicate, we do not get meaning from things, we assign meaning. In other words, whatever is out there isn't anything until we make it something. That's one explanation why your mom insists that everyone wear color-coordinated outfits when taking a family picture. The unity of color design suggests to her that your family is close and connected. Get it? If you're a guy and that doesn't make sense to you, just trust me on this and go with it. Your moms place great meaning on a lot of random things. Appreciate that she's painting a picture in her mind that makes a beautiful piece of art and she wants to include *you* in her masterpiece!

So what if your family isn't picture perfect? Join the group. My parents were divorced when I was in elementary school. I remember when the fighting started and everything seemed very wrong. My dad put a wishbone from our Thanksgiving turkey inside a picture frame with a sign that read, "Our family's wish is to stay together." I'll never forget their biggest fight to that point that resulted in a slammed door and the picture crashing to the ground from off the shaking wall. I knew it was over at that moment.

There is no "perfect" family. Every family has challenges and unique struggles. If there is a perfect family, then it's the one that pulls together in tough times and never gives up on one another. But even good people sometimes can't get along. Know that Heavenly Father placed you in your family because He knew, in His loving and infinite wisdom, that's where you could learn and grow the most. Life is a school and a test. We didn't come here to kick back and play with fuzzy bunny rabbits while drinking virgin pina coladas in the Garden of Eden. (Man, I really love virgin pina coladas—and fuzzy bunny rabbits.) We came here to learn and grow and stretch.

You really get two chances for a happy family in this life: the one you were born with and the one you create when you're married. If the first one wasn't great, then decide now to make the second one fantastic. Just because your first family experience wasn't ideal doesn't mean you're doomed to repeat those same mistakes the rest of your life and be miserable forever. Identify what *is* good about it and then build on that for your next family life. Even better, do what you can *now* to improve your family life today.

Write down . . .

What works in our family:

What doesn't work in our family:

What I can do to improve the environment in our home:

If your family life is one hot mess, cool down and make a list of the things that make you happy. Actually write them down. The list can include anything from swimming in a pool with those battery-operated pool toys that look like dolphins, to listening to Josh Groban on your bed with your eyes closed, to sipping a frozen lemonade until you get a brain freeze. (Yeah, I love all those things.) What are some things that bring happiness to your life?

Write them down here:

*

*

*

*

*

*

*

*

*

*

Focus on those things that bring a smile to your face and try to include them in your daily life. I have a list of "happy things" that I call my "Elevating Attitude Shifters." When life isn't what you hoped it would be, you can still find happiness in it. *Happiness is a choice.*

Right before I left on my mission, I read a fantastic book called *Man's Search for Meaning*. It sounds like something one of the Twelve Apostles would write, doesn't it? It was actually written by a Jewish Holocaust survivor who was in a concentration camp during World War II. He watched his fellow prisoners wither and die as everything was stripped from them: their families, their homes, their jobs, their world. He saw many of them sink into despair and give up all hope. He realized that you can have everything taken away from you except one thing: your choice to be happy. No one can force you to be unhappy. You decide.

He also learned a profound truth: when you forgive, you don't change the past—you change the future. Years later he stood face-to-face with one of the Nazi soldiers who had tormented him. He had to decide if he would let anger and bitterness swallow him up, or if he would release those poisons from him and focus on his bright future. He chose to focus on what *could* be rather than what *was*.

Never give up hope. If you think life is never going to get better, you're wrong. Hope is a very powerful thing. Sometimes it's all you're hanging on to. Keep holding on. I promise it's going to get better.

Now, if you think your life is simply too hard to be happy, allow me to introduce you to someone I know. He, of all people, had reason *not* to be happy. He was a member of a despised minority, and a citizen of an occupied country. Taxes were oppressive. Freedom was unknown. Survival was uncertain. Religion was restrictive, negative, and joyless. He was from a city reputed to be culturally deprived and morally corrupt. His followers were unlettered men with broken speech. He knew ingratitude, rejection, betrayal, misunderstanding, and murder.

By all the psychological laws of human development, Jesus should have died a judgmental, frustrated, critical, angry, unbelieving, cynical, rebellious, violence-prone, emotionally deprived, radically militant revolutionary! He could have said on the cross, "It isn't fair!" or "I'm too young to die!" or "Give me more time!" But instead, he said, "Father, into thy hands I commend my spirit."

Do we have faith and trust to put our lives and happiness in to *His* hands? Every time we suffer, *we* are on trial—will we be obedient and submissive to God's will? God's honor is also on trial. We believe *in* Jesus, but do we believe *Him*?

To Jesus every problem was a possibility in disguise. Sickness was an opportunity for healing. Sin was an opportunity for compassion. Personal abuse was an opportunity for forgiveness. Jesus wasn't depressed or overwhelmed by what the world was, but impressed and empowered into action by what the world could become.

There's a popular poster that shows a picture of Jesus and the caption: "I never said it would be easy. I only said it would be worth it." He knows the desires of our hearts and what will make us truly happy. The greatest happiness we can find is the approval of the Master.

FOR THE GUYS' EYES ONLY

In David O. McKay's book called *Secrets of a Happy Life,* he states,

> What a man is today will largely determine what he will be tomorrow. What then, should be man's greatest purposes as he marks one by one the passing years? It should be to cherish those attributes which, like his soul, will endure and brighten throughout all eternity. He should strive to drive from his life those things which will be transitory and which in the soul's progress must somewhere be discarded and rejected. More important than riches, more enduring than fame, more precious than happiness is the possession of a noble character. Truly has it been said that the grand aim of man's creation is the development of a grand character. (*Instructor*, January 1960, 1–2)

Becoming like Christ is a process, not an event. The commandments do not say, "Be ye therefore perfect by this afternoon." Chin up! You can do this!

For the Lasses with Glasses

Read the quote above in the boys' section. Substitute the word "man" and replace it with "woman." The same wise quote applies to you!

RANDOM JOKE ABOUT GLASSES

How do you make a blonde's eyes twinkle?
—Shine a light in her ear.

SUCCESS TIPS FROM MY WISE FRIENDS WHO HAVE ROSY CHEEKS, NOT ROSE-COLORED GLASSES

- Promise me you'll always remember: you're braver than you believe, and stronger than you seem and smarter than you think. —Christopher Robin to Pooh. (Yeah, I know them as personal friends.)
- Don't worry about what other people think about you. Worry about how you treat other people. —Gina Nielsen
- No matter how you feel, get up, dress up, show up, and never give up! —Barbara Smith Bailes

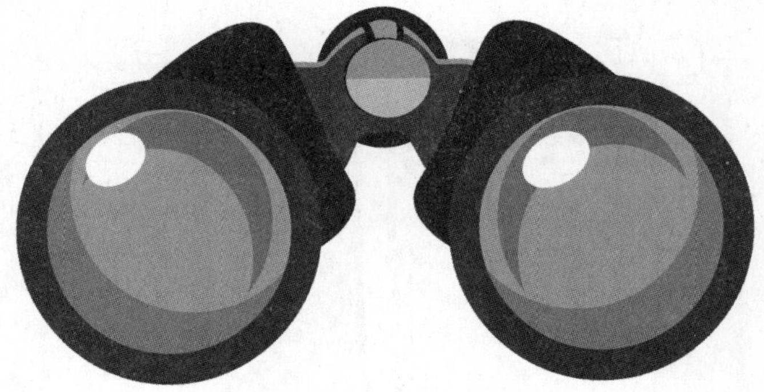

CHAPTER FIFTEEN

Binoculars: Parents and Parenting

Yeah, this is the lecture chapter. Brace yourself. Binoculars help you to see far away. Your adventure in parenting is far away, but you can start preparing for it now.

Abby McCoy, a friend of mine, once told me, "We don't just automatically become an awesome parent some day who teaches their children to read scriptures and pray—we have to start those habits ourselves in our youth before we even have a family of our own." She explained that her mantra is Richard G. Scott's quote: "We *become* what we want to *be* by consistently *being* what we want to *become* each day" ("The Transforming Power of Faith and Character," *Ensign*, Nov. 2010). That's such great advice!

When I first met her, I was extremely impressed with her wisdom at such a young age. I thought to myself, "She must have had awesome parents who taught her well." Guess who Abby's mom is? Sister Bonnie L. Oscarson, the newest general Young Women president of the entire Church!

So, here's the deal with your parents: They love you and want everything in the world for you. They want you to be happy, healthy, and successful. They've learned a few lessons about life along the way, and they want to share them with you so that you can avoid painful mistakes. I know it's annoying because you think things have changed so much since they

were teenagers running around with their pet dinosaurs. A lot of things *have* changed, but not the really important things.

They may have terrible fashion sense now, and their taste in music may appall you, but they know what things will bring enduring happiness. Because of their experiences in life, they simply interpret things differently than you do.

- **How you see a two-hundred-dollar outfit:** I'm cool and hip and hot!
- **How your parents see a two-hundred-dollar outfit:** We just worked our buns off to pay for that and the newest fad will be here in five minutes, making this new outfit obsolete.

- **How you see a bad grade:** Whatever, dude. I'll kick it up a notch next time.

- **How your parents see a bad grade**: We're failures as parents and have raised an idiot who will be forced to live on the streets and beg for food the rest of his life.

- **How you see an R-rated movie:** Everyone's talking about it, so I *have* to see it. It's not *that* bad.
- **How your parents see an R-rated movie**: My darling angel is disobeying the prophet's counsel to not watch rated R-rated movies, which means he doesn't have a testimony and will leave the Church and live eternally in the telestial kingdom.

Understand that parents have to say "no" sometimes. But why? Well, there could be a million reasons why, but here are a few to consider the next time you hear that horrible word.

They can't afford it. Life is expensive. That stinks, but it's the truth. They're probably embarrassed that they can't afford to give you everything, but they also know that even if they could afford anything your heart desired, you'd turn into a spoiled brat. Do you want to be Paris Hilton?

You don't know the full story. You want to spend the night at your friend's house, but they know that the dad is a convicted felon. I'm making this up, of course, but what if that were true? They just want to protect you.

They know it will hurt you. When you were a toddler, they'd yell "No!" when your little hand reached for the hot stove. You probably threw a tantrum because you didn't understand the danger. The same thing still applies here. Their refusal to allow you to do something may be because they know it will hurt you. It could be immediate danger or long-term danger. It could be physical danger or spiritual danger. Know that they're just trying to keep you safe. Don't throw a tantrum. They really do love you, even though it may seem like their mission in life is to make you miserable.

They're exhausted. You need a ride to your friend's house, but they simply don't have the energy. I know, that reason may seem lame, but give them a break. They're working really hard for *you*. Try to figure out another way to get a ride and suggest that option to them.

You know how *you* want to get married and have kids some day? That was your parents less than twenty years ago. Yeah, *you* were the one they dreamed about. Here are a few tips to help close the generation gap:

Talk to your parents. They *want* to be a part of your life. They love watching you grow up and can't wait to see what you do next. When you were first born, they took a gazillion pictures of you. They'd probably still do it now except they know you'd think they were being creepy stalkers if they followed you around at school taking "action" shots in your math class. By the way, accept their "friend" request on social media. I know it's annoying, but you really hurt their feelings when you shun them. They're also smart enough to be worried that you might be trying to hide something from them.

Learn about them. Ask them about their day. They used to be the center of the universe to their parents. Nowadays, hardly anyone ever asks them how things are going with them. They used to be young and cool and a part of all the action. Now they just do your laundry and drive you around everywhere. Find out what *they* are passionate about and express some interest. The more you understand how they were raised or the experiences they've had in life, the more you'll understand how they think and why they value the things they do.

Be patient with them. You think *you* are exhausted? So are your parents. Pitch in and help around the house. Parents need a break too. Have you noticed how much nicer they are when the house is clean and they've had a nap? Show them how mature you are by contributing. Be a blessing to them, not a burden.

Forgive them. When you were born, you didn't come with an instruction manual. If you're the oldest child—whoa! Baby! They're trying to figure everything out. Sorry that you're the guinea pig. Let them know when they've done something right with their newly developed parenting skills. Carefully suggest other options if what they're doing isn't helping you. They really do *want* to be good parents. If you disagree with a decision they make, state a clear case with logical reasons and ask them to reconsider. They may not change their mind, but now you've proven to them that you're maturing and looking at all sides of the issue.

Consider their advice. If they don't like your boyfriend or girlfriend, it's for a reason. Yeah, they won't think anyone is ever going to be good enough for you, but if they're protesting especially loudly about the person you're dating, then pay attention. They know how difficult marriage is and they must see some red flags that you're simply not noticing. Your natural response will be, "But they don't know him like I do." That's true, but something is causing them to worry and you should find out what that is.

Tell them what you need. If you want to chill in your bedroom after school because you need your space, let them know that there is nothing wrong and that you just need to decompress before you start on homework and chores. If you want something, tell them what you're willing to do to earn it. Create a contract with them if you have to. Explain *why* you need something rather than just asking for it. That doesn't necessarily mean you'll get it, but it helps them to understand what's going on in your brain. They don't want to raise a kid who just expects the world to give them a handout for no effort on their part.

Try to understand that they were once newlyweds with big hopes and dreams for their future children. They held you in their arms as a new, sweet baby dressed in pink or blue, and imagined the great things you would do in the world. They knew you would do tremendous things because, after all, you are their child! They know you have your agency, but they still have their dreams for you. So when they imagine you receiving the Nobel Peace Prize or graduating from Harvard with honors, give them a break! Like Heavenly Father, they love you and expect the best *for* you and *from* you. The reason they lecture about how your life should be lived is because they want yours to be *better* than theirs. They want you to be better than they are!

COOL IDEA

Here's an idea to try if talking to your parents results in everyone fuming and storming out of the room in frustration. Create a "pillow talk book." Put a little notebook under their pillow and explain to them that you want to share conversations in writing. You can write a question or make a comment to get them started. Once they've answered your question in the notebook, they are supposed to put the notebook under your pillow. You then write another question or comment and keep the notebook going back and forth. For some parents and teens, it's much easier to communicate when they have time to carefully consider their thoughts. It's kind of fun to see what each person writes.

THE WEIRDEST THING EVER

You're going to grow up and hear words come out of your mouth that your parents said to you. As you age, you're even going to start to look more like them. Eww. Gross, right? When you thought it would never happen, you're going to realize that you've become your parents. *People say you don't truly appreciate your parents until you are one or bury one.*

FOR THE GUYS' EYES ONLY

If you want to know what a girl is going to be like in thirty years, meet her parents. She may physically look like them when she ages, but she may also share their values, habits, and behaviors. That could be a good thing or bad thing, depending on her parents! It doesn't mean she *will* be like them. She has her agency, but you can't argue too much with genes.

Some couples get engaged without ever meeting each other's parents, thinking, "It doesn't matter what they're like because we're in love!" I hate to break it to you, but it's kind of a package deal. Her parents are going to want you to spend Christmas with them. Her siblings are going to be sitting next to you at Thanksgiving dinner every year. They may want to go on vacations with you every summer or even move next door to you. You need to see the whole package before you decide to make it a part of your life forever. You really do marry the family. Make sure you like them, because you'll be dealing with them for the rest of your life.

So, are you ready to be a father right now? No? Then stop thinking about sex. Don't even think about sneaking a peek at pornography, fooling yourself that you can look once and it won't really matter. You will *never* be able to look just once. I know teenage boys and grown adult men who struggle daily with the guilt and pain of getting hooked on that garbage. It destroys relationships and it can destroy you.

You say you want to marry a lovely girl in the temple who will be a beautiful wife and loving mother, and then you look at that trash? It's so offensive to what a real woman is. If you're not ready to be a father right now, then don't do the things that result in your being a father right now. Too blunt?

For the Lasses with Glasses

Once, when I was serving as a Young Women leader, we decided to invite some guest speakers to talk the young men and young women about the law of chastity. The youth leaders were too embarrassed to talk about such things, so we figured we'd bring in the experts to do it for us. We invited the mission president to talk with the young men in a separate room, and then we had a sweet, old lady from LDS Social Services speak to the young women in another room. I had just had a new baby, so I spent quite a bit of time that night walking the halls, trying to keep my baby happy and quiet.

I'll never forget the contrast of what I heard when I peeked into both rooms. The mission president was saying all those "scary" words and telling the young men exactly what was expected of them. He told them the things they were definitely not allowed to do in order to be chaste and worthy to hold the priesthood, and to have the honor of serving a mission. You know all that stuff, right? No pornography! No masturbation! No sex! My sensitive ears were burning, but I was grateful that he was being clear and honest with our dear young men.

Then, when I walked by the room where all of our precious young women were seated, I heard the old lady kindly whisper, "Should you find yourself pregnant . . ." Wait. What? How do you "*find* yourself pregnant"? As if you suddenly noticed and had no idea how that happened? I thought she did such a disservice to our young women that night. The girls needed to hear all of those same "scary" and uncomfortable words about sex that the young men were hearing. It takes two to tango, you know.

You cute girls have no idea the affect you have on guys. I remember the day when I started to catch on. When I was in middle school I sat next to a guy I thought was super hot in my typing class. Back then we called it typing, but it was a basic keyboarding class for "newbs." I'll bet most of you started playing around on computer keyboards when you were two! Anyway, I wore a skirt to school one day and I remember how the cute guy stopped and stared at me for what seemed like an awkward eternity. Finally, he wiped the saliva off his mouth (I'm completely exaggerating for the sake of drama here) and said, "Wow! Look at those legs!" (That part I didn't exaggerate. He really said that.) I had no idea what he was talking about. I mean, legs. Legs? I remember going home at the end of the school day and staring at my legs in a full-length mirror to see what was wrong with them.

Their hormones make them go crazy thinking about you. You have no idea. Help them to think pure thoughts by dressing modestly. Don't tease them by trying to act like a sexy supermodel. I have four boys and they *all* agree that they appreciate it more when you help them to be good. They admire you *way* more when you dress modestly and respect your own body. I'm not making this up. They begged me to remind you to be pure and chaste, and not be like the world. The world needs you to be good and kind and clean and true.

RANDOM JOKE ABOUT GLASSES

What kind of music do people who need to wear glasses listen to?
—iTunes

SUCCESS TIPS FROM MY WISE FRIENDS WHO ARE GREAT PARENTS

* Your life is about more than just today. Make choices now that you'll be happy you made when you're thirty, forty, and older. —Tristi Pinkston (She's a kind friend who writes awesome historical fiction. Take a look at her books at www.TristiPinkston.com.)
* You think your parents are so much older than you, but it was only a few years ago that they were your age. The older you get, the less their age difference is going to seem to you. They're on the same journey of life that you are, but just a few steps ahead. Appreciate that they've learned a few things and want to share those lessons with you so that you don't have to make the same mistakes. —Sheila Whittaker

CHAPTER SIXTEEN

Mr. Potato Head Glasses: Where's Your Focus?

Why Mr. Potato Head glasses? Try putting them on. What happens? They squeeze your face so hard that, before long, the uncomfortable pain is all you can think about it. You become completely focused on one thing. It's kind of weird that I know that, right?

I like to write inspiring quotes on slips of paper and put them in my son's lunch every day before he leaves for school so he will be focused on good things. I think it's a loving gesture. He thinks I'm weird. Here are some of the thoughts I try to keep on my mind at all times:

- We give our lives to that which we give our time.
- If you focus on the negative, you will be conquered by every person, circumstance, and situation.
- Every minute you are angry you lose sixty seconds of happiness.
- Work in your garden when you're angry because it puts you in your place: on your knees.
- The shortest distance between a problem and a solution is the distance between your knees and the floor.
- The happiest people don't necessarily have the best of everything. They just make the best of everything they have.

- Life isn't about how to survive the storm, but how to dance in the rain.
- We are not mortal beings having spiritual experiences, but spiritual beings having a mortal experience.

When I was a student at BYU, Elder Jeffrey R. Holland was the president of the university. We used to sing "Jeffrey wants me for a zoobie!" to the tune of "Jesus Wants Me for a Sunbeam." BYU students used to be called zoobies. Okay, the joke is losing its steam when I have to explain everything about it. Moving on.

I remember sitting in a fireside where President Holland spoke about expanding our vision so that we could see the big picture. He described our premortal existence as Act I of a play. He said, "You were brilliant there! You learned and excelled in various areas that would bless your life in Act II: Earth Life." Writers introduce their characters in Act I, but in Act II the actors go through tests, trials, temptations, and sometimes tragedy. Nowhere in Act II does it say "happily ever after." That doesn't happen until Act III. We're so focused on our mortal existence now that we forget this isn't the whole story.

I wrote in my fireside notes that night, "You cannot go back and have a brandnew start, my friend. But you can start over right now and create a brandnew end!" If you don't like how your life is going right now, change it. Another quote I like is by Carl Bard:

> It's only the view from where you sit
> that makes you feel defeat.
> Life is full of many aisles, so
> Why don't you change your seat!

Elder Holland then switched his analogy to a football game and said, "The victory has already been posted on the scoreboard. We know who wins. The strange thing is we're all standing on the field, trying to decide which jersey to wear." Which side do you want to be on? Still trying to decide? Let me help you by gathering some facts. You've probably read the scripture, "Wherefore by their fruits ye shall know them" (Matthew 7:20). What exactly does that mean? It means you can test something by seeing the results it gives.

Fill in the consequences of these actions:

Study hard in school. Result:

Become addicted to meth. Result:

Work hard at a job. Result:

Run away from home. Result:

Believe in a loving God. Result:

Don't believe in life after death. Result:

Living a life of integrity. Result:

Not caring about other people. Result:

Are the results obvious or hard to see? If you lived an obedient, faithful life of devotion to God, what would the fruits be? How would your life be better if you didn't?

I asked Jenny Oaks Baker to send me some advice to share with you in this book. She's an extremely accomplished violinist and is as beautiful on the inside as she is on the outside. (Check out her YouTube channel!) This is what she wanted you to know:

> There is *nothing* that the world has to offer that can compare to what the Lord would like to bless you with. I have been nominated for a Grammy and walked the red carpet. Pretty cool as far as the things of the world go, but that experience is *nothing* compared to the glorious feeling of worthily walking the white carpets in the Lord's House. Do *not* risk losing the blessings that the Lord has in store for each of you! Keep yourselves morally clean and unspoiled from the world! You do not want to miss out on your divine destiny!

Pretty awesome, right? One of the wonderful things about going to the temple is that it helps us **SEE** the world better. I live in Las Vegas where the temple is high on a hill overlooking "Sin City." People get so easily lost in the glitz and glamour of the famous Las Vegas Strip below. When people

look at all of the casinos, nightclubs, and bars that call to them with neon lights and promises of riches, it's easy to be mesmerized. When I look down on all of it from the temple grounds, it seems so ridiculous and fleeting.

One of my sons had a friend visiting in town so I drove them all over the Strip, showing off some of the beautiful hotels with impressive dancing water fountains and fancy restaurants. We drove past a dumpy casino and I commented how there was a much nicer place around the corner. My son, in his great wisdom and humor, said, "Mom, they're all a bunch of gold-encrusted turds." He was right. I was trying to make the casinos seem so great, but in the end, they were all just casinos, places where gullible customers lose their money and dreams.

When you take an eye exam, the doctor has you stand back and focus on one letter at a time, right? To help you improve your eternal vision, stand back from the world and focus on the temple. Fill your mind with inspiring thoughts and quotes. Memorize some. Keep an "Inspiring Quotes Journal." Remember that what's happening right now in your life is only a small part of the story.

Mr. Potato Head Glasses

Perspective is how we see things from where we are. Eternal perspective is the way God sees things! Our perspective may change, depending upon our experiences and circumstances. The teachings of the gospel and the influence of the Spirit can help us begin to see things as God sees them—from an eternal perspective. We can view our present mortal life as a short, but significant, part of eternity. "All things . . . are manifest, past, present, and future, and are continually before the Lord" (D&C 130:7).

By viewing our lives from the perspective of eternity, we realize that the difficulties we face in mortality are transitory. The Lord told the suffering Joseph Smith, "My son, peace be unto thy soul; thine adversity and thine afflictions shall be but a small moment; and then, if thou endure it well, God shall exalt thee on high; thou shalt triumph over all thy foes" (D&C 121:7–8). Let go. Let God.

RANDOM JOKE ABOUT GLASSES

"Doctor! Doctor, I need glasses!"

"You certainly do, ma'am. This is a barber shop."

SUCCESS TIPS FROM MY WISE FRIENDS WHO ARE FOCUSED ON WHAT IS TRULY IMPORTANT IN LIFE

- Don't give up what you want most for what you want today. —Roger Hayes
- Life is a journey and no matter what mountains and forests your path may go through, your Father in Heaven will *always* hold his arms open for your return. —Josi Kilpack (Have you seen the covers of her books? They always have super yummy looking food on them with dessert food titles. That makes them sound like cookbooks, but they're really fun mysteries, not cookbooks. I just want to eat her books. Did you know she didn't even like reading until her mom gave her a novel to read when she was thirteen. Now she's an award-winning author and friend. You can check her books out at www.josiskilpack.com.)
- If you think you can, you're right! —Traci Schull Heppler
- Above anything, be honest with yourself and people that you deal with. Love yourself and your family. —Jennifer Smith El Alami

CHAPTER SEVENTEEN

Tanning Goggles: See Your Light

I confess, I've been to tanning salons. When I was younger, I wanted to look tan and sporty, even though I was stuck inside a building working all day in a dark office. It's really bad for you, so I don't recommend it. (I mean tanning. Come to think of it, so is working all day in a dark office.) I don't go to tanning salons anymore and am proud of my pasty-white complexion. Make sure your mom reads this paragraph so she knows I'm not encouraging you to go. I don't want to get on her bad side.

Before I would lie down on the cancerous bed of lights, I would put on tanning goggles to protect my eyes from the harmful rays. (Gee, you'd think that having to put on protective gear would have been my first clue that this was bad for my body, right?) If I opened my eyes, I couldn't really see anything, except for a bright light.

Now, this is a mediocre analogy, but work with me people—I'm trying to stick with this glasses theme here. Sometimes we don't have a clear life vision. Very few teenagers have a life plan written down. Do you? We all know that Jesus is the Light of the World and He can help us see more clearly. Can you feel His light on you?

Did you know that a sunflower always turns its face to the sun? By evening, the sunflower has turned its position and faces the setting sun. We need to turn our face to the Son. "And seek the face of the Lord always" (D&C 101:38). A poem by an unkown author reads,

Tanning Goggles

The man whispered,
"God, speak to me."
And a meadowlark sang.
But the man did not hear.
So the man yelled, "God speak to me!"
And the thunder rolled across the sky.
But the man did not listen.
The man looked around and said,
"God let me see you."
And a star shone brightly.
But the man did not notice.
And the man shouted,
"God show me a miracle!"
And a life was born.
But the man did not know.
So the man cried out in despair,
"Touch me God and let me know that you are here!"
Whereupon God reached down and touched the man.
But the man brushed the butterfly away and walked on.

You were sent here to learn and grow. You have a unique mission. Only you can do it. Do you know what it is?

"Your task, to build a better world," God said.
I answered, "How? The world is such a large vast place,
so complicated now.
And I so small and useless am. There's nothing I can do."
But God in all His wisdom said, "Just build a better you."
(N. Eldon Tanner, "Going Forth to Serve,"*BYU Speeches,* 30 Jan 1979)

But how? What *is* my life mission? What is my unique purpose? Well, if you're still alive, you haven't completed it yet! We've all asked that question, or at least we should. The Lord has given us some tools to use to figure out the answer:

- The scriptures—Life is an open book test. The resources are the scriptures.
- Your patriarchal blessing—A love letter from the Lord that reminds you of who you truly are and can be.
- The Holy Ghost—Be in tune and you will be led in the right direction. Listen to your head and your heart. What are they telling you?

* Priesthood blessings—They can help you not become distracted. Ask for one at the beginning of each school year and before big decisions in your life.

When I teach my BYU–I students online, there is a lesson plan that teaches them how to set effective goals. They are called S.M.A.R.T. goals. Here is what each letter stands for:

* S = Specific. (What exactly do you want to accomplish?)
* M = Measurable. (How will you know if you've reached your goal?)
* A = Attainable. (Aim for something big, but make sure it's possible.)
* R = Realistic. (Are you willing and able to accomplish it?)
* T = Time. (Create a time frame of when you will start and finish.)

Outline one goal you want to reach in the next six months:

S =

M =

A =

R =

T =

Your S.M.A.R.T. goal should be able to identify the big "W" questions: Who, What, Where, When, and Why. If you have a clear vision, you're more likely to reach your goal.

Don't miss out on a blessing because it isn't packaged the way you expect. When our life doesn't go according to our plans, we often fail to see the Lord's hand in the change. I have a son who has always worried that he needs to be in the right place at the right time in order for the Lord to work through Him. If you're doing what you're supposed to be doing, the Lord will *place* you where He needs you.

Elder Richard G. Scott said, "When your life complies with the will of the Lord and is in harmony with His teachings, the Holy Ghost is your companion in need. You will be able to be inspired by the Lord to know what to do. When needed, your efforts will be fortified with divine power. . . . You can be protected and strengthened to do what alone would be impossible" ("Trust in the Lord," *Ensign*, May 1989). Isn't that an awesome promise?

President Gordon B. Hinckley assured us, "God is weaving his tapestry according to his own grand design. All flesh is in his hands. It is not our prerogative to counsel him. It is our responsibility and our opportunity to be at peace in our minds and in our hearts, and to know that he is God, that this is his work, and that he will not permit it to fail" ("He Slumbers Not, Nor Sleeps," *Ensign*, May 1983).

There was a couple looking for a new town to move to. They drove around and saw a man standing on a street corner. As they rolled down the car window, they asked him what he thought of the town. The man answered by asking them, "What was your old town like?" They only had terrible things to say about where they were moving from and that they were too happy to be leaving. The man answered, "You'll find the same thing here."

You see what you're looking for. An apple looks different to Picasso than to the grocer or even Steve Jobs because their visual matrices are different. When you look at yourself, do you see who you are now or who you could be? Focus on that future person and start acting that way now. Before you know it, you will actually *be* that person.

Once upon a time, there were six wise men who lived together in a small town. The six wise men were blind. One day, an elephant was brought to the town. The six men wanted to see the elephant, but how could they? "I know," said the first man. "We will feel him!"

"Good idea," said the others. "Then we'll know what an elephant is like."

So the six men went to see the elephant. The first one touched the elephant's big, flat ear. He felt it move slowly back and forth.

"The elephant is like a fan," the first man cried.

The second man felt the elephant's legs. "He's like a tree," he cried.

"You're both wrong," said the third man. "The elephant is like a rope." This man was feeling the elephant's tail.

Just then the fourth man pricked his hand on the elephant's sharp tusk. "The elephant is like a spear!" he cried.

"No, no," cried the fifth man. "He's like a high wall." While he spoke he felt the elephant's side.

The sixth man was holding the elephant's trunk. "You're all wrong," he said. "The elephant is like a snake."

"No, no, like a rope!" "Snake!" "Wall!" "You're wrong!" "I'm right!" The six blind men shouted at each other. Who was right?

FOR THE GUYS' EYES ONLY

In a talk given by President David O. McKay in June 1965, he outlined the order in which the priesthood brethren will be asked by Jesus Christ to give an accounting of their stewardships:

* An accounting of our relationship with our spouse

- An individual account of relationships with each child
- The development of personal talents
- The fulfillment of Church assignments
- How honest we were with our dealings
- An accounting of our contributions to the community

Seek ye first the kingdom of God.

RANDOM JOKE ABOUT GLASSES

What did the right eye say to the left eye?

—Between you and me, there's something that smells.

SUCCESS TIPS FROM MY WISE FRIENDS WHO KNOW WHO THEY ARE

- Enjoy all what you make and make all with love. —Rosshanti F. Caslol
- Question everything, especially assumed authority, including your own. —Alex Rice (He's my talented cousin who plays the piano in two tribute bands!)
- Always remember, perception is reality. —Richard Fritzler
- Don't settle for something because you are afraid nothing else better will come along. Don't give up and keep on trucking! If you settle, you will not be happy. —Jennifer Meuter Parry
- Attitude is everything! You don't *have* to; you *get* to! A good attitude goes a long way in life and helps you push through the hard things. —Chris Jensen

CHAPTER EIGHTEEN

Eye Patch: It's Only a Flesh Wound

Sometimes we go through experiences in life that leave wounds. The eye patch represents trials we go through in life—or even our sins—that leave a mark. Face it, we're all going to show up in heaven with lots of spiritual bumps and bruises from having gone through this mortal experience. None of us is getting out of here alive.

We shouted for joy when hearing the plan of happiness (Job 38:7) even though we knew that trials and tests were part of the package deal. We were *still* glad and excited about coming here! Adam and Eve left the Garden of Eden "that they might have *joy*," not days of constant leisure, yawning and lounging in front of the TV for eternity (2 Nephi 2:25; italics added). Trials are a central part of mortal life. It's how we learn and grow and *become*. Get used to it!

We don't always understand why bad things happen, but you should know that it's for a reason. We usually don't know why until *after* we've gone through it. When you're right in the middle of a trial or challenge, ask Heavenly Father to teach you what it is you're supposed to be learning. That sometimes speeds up the process so that you can get through it faster! You don't want to just *survive* a trial, but thrive because of it. Tree branches either break off in a storm or become stronger. Choose to become stronger because of your challenges. It doesn't matter what the challenges are, but who you become because of them.

Eye Patch

Obedience doesn't guarantee smooth sailing, but it can definitely help us avoid serious problems. For example, if you obey the Word of Wisdom, you are *guaranteed* to never get addicted to drugs, alcohol, or cigarettes! When you are doing what you are supposed to do, like attending church and studying your scriptures and praying, you will have a feeling of peace, even if you are going through difficult times. God can turn your trials into a foundation of strength.

Kids your age often have a lot of stress. You have a lot going on in your life and have to learn how to manage it all: school, work, family, church, friends, and developing talents. A lot is riding on how well you do in school, for example, because it can determine whether you go on to college or end up serving French fries for the rest of your life. Failure is a big fear for a lot of you. How do you cope?

I have some good news and some bad news for you. The bad news: that's life! You will always have a lot of things to juggle. Finding balance is one of the challenges you'll face every day on this earth. The good news: that's life! Enjoy it! Isn't it wonderful that you have so many interesting and exciting things going on?

The trick is to figure out how to remain sane through it all and to enjoy the journey. You can't just wish things were different; you have to have a strategy. What's yours?

Strategy #1: Use a daily planner.

Do you have one? It can be a paper planner you keep in your purse or wallet. Old school, right? That's what missionaries use! It could also be a digital planner you keep on your phone like Google Calendar. You need to get organized. The hours of the day will fly by whether you have a plan or not. If you're not careful, the hours will disappear without you accomplishing anything. It's amazing how fast time flies when you're watching YouTube videos or playing video games. Before you know it, your parents are asking you why you still haven't finished your homework or washed the dishes. Plan what needs to be done and do those things *first.* It's like a financial budget—it requires discipline, but you'll be happy with the results if you stick to it. I always tell my kids that playtime is sweeter when you don't have homework and chores still hanging over your head.

Strategy #2: Eat a whale.

How do you eat a whale? One bite at a time. (You don't have to really eat a whale . . . it's a metaphor, folks!) Identify your long-term goals and then break them into smaller steps that you can work on each day, a little at a time. Do you have dreams of being a concert pianist? Fantastic! Then set your timer and practice thirty minutes a day. Okay, if you're going to be a professional pianist, it's probably going to require a lot more time than that! Do you want to be a famous entrepreneur? Great! Then write down on your daily planner a time when you can research what other entrepreneurs did to succeed. The point is to stop dreaming and actually include the steps you need to take to reach your goals into your daily life. Knowing that you're truly working on what's important to you each day will give you such an empowering feeling, as well as the talents to make your dreams come true.

Strategy #3: Learn how to constructively blow off steam.

Yelling at your family and freaking out aren't the best techniques for dealing with stress. I teach cooking students at Le Cordon Bleu who have chosen a profession that requires them to be on their feet in hot, loud kitchens under serious deadlines to produce a finished product. It's extremely stressful. Tempers flare and bad language spews out of their mouths. You've probably seen one of those cooking shows where the head chef yells at everyone, right? I really hate that. Many people in that industry are chain smokers because they only get short breaks and need to find some way to quickly diffuse the pressure. You need to find better ways to chill. What works for you? Chewing gum? Doing yoga? Shooting some hoops? Listening to music? Painting your toenails?

Make a "Go To" list here that you can use when you're ready to explode:

-
-
-
-

Strategy #4: Look in the mirror.

Scary, right? Ask yourself where the stress is really coming from. Are you the one putting all of the pressure on yourself or is it someone else? Are the demands realistic? Are you killing yourself because you think everything has to be perfect? It doesn't, you know. Someone once said, "Don't sweat the small stuff." If something isn't going to matter in five years, then don't worry so much about it. Focus on the things that really count. If you're stressing out because of what others want, then talk to them about their expectations. If it's your parents, then find out what you can all do *together* to accomplish the desired tasks. You don't have to do it all alone. Your parents *want* you to succeed and should be willing to help you get there. If it's your friends who are pressuring you, stop and analyze if what they want is what you truly want. You'll never be happy if you're constantly trying to live up to others' expectations. What do *you* want? If you want to win that competition, then quit your whining and do what it takes to be the best. Know that excellence requires a price. Are you willing to pay it?

Strategy #5: Be Dory.

Did you ever see the movie *Finding Nemo*? It's one of the greatest Disney movies ever. Dory is the name of a royal blue tang fish who sings the little mantra "just keep swimming." It's simple and it's actually really great advice. Just keep going. When you're working hard and want to give up, just keep going. When you're tired and can't see the finish line, just keep going. When you're depressed and don't feel like doing what you're supposed to anymore, just keep going. Eventually, you're going to get through it and the reward may be closer than you think. Mark Twain said, "Keep away from people who try to belittle your ambitions. Small people always do that, but the really great make you feel that you, too, can become great."

Strategy #6: Remember all of the "Sunday School answers."

The answers to almost every question your Sunday School teacher will ask you are:

- The Atonement of Jesus Christ
- Study the scriptures
- Prayer
- Keep the commandments
- The gospel has been restored

When you're going through struggles and challenges, remember to pray. Search the scriptures more. Be faithful in keeping your covenants. Repent. Live the gospel. It really is that simple.

The Lord is always there. *We* choose the distance between ourselves and Him. Because of the Fall, we aren't in the presence of God anymore. We can't speak to Him face-to-face like Adam did, but we can have a relationship with Him still and feel close, even with all that distance. The gospel of Jesus Christ is the great means by which we can do that. I am so grateful for that truth.

Going through trials and challenges in life also helps you understand others who are going through difficult times as well. The only way to have true empathy for someone's pain is to have felt it yourself. That's why Jesus came to earth, that He might "know according to the flesh how to succor his people according to their infirmities" (Alma 7:12).

I used to think that the Atonement was really meant for people who committed terrible sins so that they could repent and try again. I wasn't planning on robbing any banks or killing anyone, so I didn't fully grasp the depth of what the Savior had done for me. It wasn't until I was a young mother when I finally appreciated the part of the Atonement that applied directly to me. I had just lost a baby and my heart was broken. Both my spirit and body grieved for the loss of my little one. I could hardly function and spent days in a dark depression. One afternoon, while I was listening to a church talk to try to calm my tormented soul, I felt the Savior's loving arms embrace me. No, I didn't feel His actual arms, but I *knew* He was right there next to me. I felt an overwhelming sense of love and peace. I knew that everything would be okay and that the Savior knew me, loved me, and was sad with me. The cleansing tears began to flow down my cheeks. It changed everything for me.

I suddenly remembered that part of the Atonement included the pains of the world that Jesus experienced in the Garden of Gethsemane, which were so great that He bled from every pore. He suffered for all of our sins, but He also felt the weight of our troubles and sorrow from mortality . . . even those *not* connected with sin. He understood fully what it feels like to be mortal. I realized that Jesus *knew* exactly how I was feeling, because He had felt it already before me. His Atonement washes over sins *and* the tears of mortal living. For the first time, the Atonement became very real to me. I knew He could heal my heart and make my burden light. He was the only one who could do it.

I had greater empathy and understanding for others who had lost their babies. I loved the children I did have even more. I wanted to be better. My trial seemed to shorten the distance between me and my Heavenly Father. I became instantly focused on what truly mattered in life. Would I wish that pain on anyone? Absolutely not, but I recognize the importance of the trial in teaching me some important lessons in life.

Resolve to get rid of any problems or faults that separate you from God. Repent. Just do it. I'm sure that'll be on Nike's new shoe ad during the Millennium. If you're headed in the wrong direction, God allows U-turns. I lived in Georgia (the Bible Belt in the South) for years where churches put signs outside their buildings to try to entice people to come in and check them out. Some read:

- In the dark? Follow the Son.
- If you can't sleep, don't count sheep. Talk to the Shepherd.
- Forbidden fruit creates many jams.
- This is a CH - - CH. What is missing? U R!
- Do not wait for the hearse to take you to church.
- If you don't like the way you were born, try being born again.

There is a big difference between repenting and feeling badly for mistakes we've made and just feeling badly because we got caught. There is also a difference between feeling sorrow for our sins and feeling true "godly" sorrow when we know we have hurt Heavenly Father because of our disobedience. When we sin, we're simply removing ourselves from God. He's not the one who moved away. We are! Godly sorrow is when we recognize the pain we've caused Him because of our choices to move away from Him.

There is a somewhat famous story about Leonardo da Vinci that illustrates how many of his paintings were truly inspired by God. Some children were visiting the famous artist one day when one of them accidentally knocked over a stack of canvases. This upset the master artist because he had been working very quietly and sensitively. He instantly became angry, threw his brush on the floor, and hurled some harsh words to the frightened little boy, who ran crying from the studio. Leonardo, now alone again, tried to continue his work. He was trying to paint the face of Jesus on the canvas that would become the famous work of art known as "The Last Supper," but he couldn't do it. His creativity had stopped.

Leonardo da Vinci put down his brush and went out into the streets and alleys until he found the little boy. He said, "I'm sorry, little one. I shouldn't have spoken so harshly. Forgive me, even as Christ forgives. I have done something worse than you. You only knocked over the canvases, but I, in my anger, blocked the flow of God into my life. Will you come back with me?" He took the boy back into the studio with him. They smiled as the face of Jesus came quite naturally from the master's brush. That face has been an inspiration to millions ever since.

Focusing on others steadily bathes us with inspiration, motivation, and perspective. Whenever we are going through trials or feeling distanced from Heavenly Father, one of the best things we can do to get our groove back is to serve. Happiness lies within us paradoxically as we reach out to what is outside of us. Happiness is not what you *get* but what you *give.*

When I was going to BYU, I was the student director at a night school for handicapped adults. Some of the people I taught there were physically handicapped, but most of them were mentally handicapped and had severe learning disabilities. They lived in group homes where they had help with their everyday tasks, and they were attending this night school to learn skills that would allow them to get a simple job in the community. I volunteered there twice a week and loved it. It was fun to teach the handicapped students and I felt like I was doing something truly meaningful to help other people. After my second year of volunteering there, I often found myself frustrated because the students didn't seem to progress and I wondered if I was wasting my time. Even worse, I was in charge of all the other BYU student volunteers and worried that I might be wasting their time as well.

I was a busy college student with my own challenges and I worried that the time I spent volunteering at the school would be better spent studying for my exams. I always felt great after serving at the school and knew it was good for me to have a mental break from my books. But was I really doing any good and making any real difference there?

One Saturday morning, my parents came to town and took me out to breakfast. That was a real treat and I was thrilled to spend a little bit of time with them. While we were eating, I noticed one of my mentally handicapped students sitting all alone at a table nearby. I walked over and gave him a big hug. I asked him what he was doing there and he informed me that it was his birthday. I was sad to see him sitting all by himself on such a special occasion, but he explained that he wanted to see if he could go to a restaurant by himself, order, and be like a "normal" person. He said that he been inspired by our night classes together and he was challenging himself to become better. My heart was so touched. I felt so much love for him, as well as for my Heavenly Father, who allowed me to serve such special people. My problems were never as large as I felt they were. I finally realized that we don't serve others to necessarily change the world, but to change ourselves.

FOR THE GUYS' EYES ONLY

You will have burdens placed upon you in this life simply because you're a man. You are to be the provider and protector in your family. Those are big responsibilities. Juggling all of the demands of work, home, Church, and everything else will be frustrating, unless you allow the Lord to help you. Your wife and your children will look to you for priesthood leadership. You won't have time to quickly repent and suddenly make yourself worthy when someone needs a priesthood blessing. Be ready all of the time.

Your priesthood gives you great power. Like Spider-Man says, "With great power comes great responsibility." Use your priesthood power wisely and carefully. It is a power to serve others. It is the very same power that Jesus Christ used to heal the sick, raise the dead, and create this world. It is predicated upon your faithfulness. In other words, if you don't work, it won't either. Work to be valiant and true at all times.

For the Lasses with Glasses

Some of your deepest heartaches and challenges will be associated with your female body. Girls are terribly hard on themselves when they look in the mirror. You will probably never think you're pretty enough because society and Hollywood constantly parade Photoshopped images in front of you about what they think is the "beauty of the day." What the mirror isn't telling you is how smart, kind, and funny you are, and a million other qualities you possess inside. Be kind to yourself.

Your body was designed to co-create with God. What an amazing miracle that is! No wonder Satan tries so hard to get us to misuse our bodies. When I was a Young Women president several years ago, my bishop confided in me and sadly said, "Some of these girls are just giving it away." Do you know what "it" is? It's that incredible gift you've been given by a loving Father in Heaven that makes you attractive to boys and allows you to create life. Boys have been given the priesthood as a power to bless others and serve. Girls have also been given a power that blesses others with life. Like the boys, you must use that power *very* carefully and wisely. Isn't it interesting that both gifts are designed to help other people? Heavenly Father is so smart!

RANDOM JOKE ABOUT GLASSES

What was the lens's excuse to the policeman?
—I've been framed!

SUCCESS TIPS FROM MY WISE FRIENDS WHO HAVE LEARNED ABOUT THE SAVIOR THROUGH TRIALS AND SERVICE

- Comedian Jonathan Winters always made me laugh and think. He said, "I couldn't wait for success, so I went ahead without it." —Janet Kay Jensen (She's a sweet friend who has written sweet books you can see at www.kayjensen.com.)
- No matter what troubles come in your life, hold onto the greatness inside you. God needs you to share it with the world. —Ronda Hinrichsen (She is a great writer of some very creative books. She also writes under a pen name, but I'm not allowed to tell you what that is. You can find her at rondahinrichsen.com.)
- My twin sister, Tracey Long, shares this tip: Each person must decide for themselves what their definition of success is for their own life. Because we each have been given a unique set of talents, gifts, and

challenges, only *you* can determine if you have truly reached your true divine potential. A simple checklist you can remember to help you "win daily" is:

W—Work
I—Improve yourself
N—Nurture your health

D—Daily divine dialog
A—Action toward your goals
I—Instrument for good
L—Love someone
Y—Yearn to learn

CHAPTER NINETEEN

Old Granny Glasses: Life Is Shorter than You Think

I felt like I was eleven years old forever. I couldn't wait to be a part of the Young Women program and not have to sing with the Primary children in sacrament meeting anymore. I was the tallest kid and would try to duck down a little bit so it wasn't so obvious that I was in my awkward-gigantic phase and not one of those adorable little Sunbeams collapsed over the front podium receiving *oohs* and *aahs* from the adoring parents in the congregation.

Well, you're not in Primary anymore! You're now in one of the most exciting phases of your life. *The decisions you make in the next few years will determine the quality of the rest of your life.* You even get to order for yourself at a restaurant now. Yep, you're in the big leagues. A word of caution: don't be in such a hurry to grow up; you'll be an adult *forever*, but you're only going to be a kid for a few short years. Always stay young at heart! I tried to be a normal adult once. Worst two minutes of my life.

Here are a few more signs you're getting older and wiser:

- Your parents stop sounding stupid.
- You start remembering to do your chores without being reminded.
- You've stopped bullying your little siblings and actually have fun with them now.

- ✳ All your homework gets done. All the time.
- ✳ You read a book and it made you think.
- ✳ You've made friends with a geek.
- ✳ You can sit through one hour of educational television without wanting to fall asleep.
- ✳ You've asked for a raise in your allowance and explained why, and your parents agreed.
- ✳ Your body is changing so fast that your best friend doesn't recognize you.
- ✳ You've realized that you probably will never become a cowboy or Superman.
- ✳ You can sip through a straw without being tempted to blow bubbles in your drink.
- ✳ Candy doesn't taste as good as it used to, and you find yourself ordering salads in restaurants.
- ✳ You've walked away from a fight because the argument was stupid.

Mark Twain said, "Age is an issue of mind over matter. If you don't mind, it doesn't matter!" Right now anyone four years older than you seems really old, and your parents seem ancient. When you're a freshman in high school, a senior seems so old and wise. You can't even imagine what it would feel like to be fifty. Yikes! I remember when I was your age hearing old people say, "Twenty years ago I . . ." and the whole time I was thinking "EEK! I haven't even been alive for twenty years!"

What's interesting is that the older you get, the less important age differences are. I still feel like a teenager, but my body says otherwise. I'm also starting to think that my house is haunted. Every time I look in my mirror a crazy old lady stands in front of me so that I can't see my reflection!

Old Granny Glasses

Just think, you might have been best friends with your parents in the premortal existence, hanging out and taking classes together to prepare for earth life. Maybe they volunteered to come down here first so that you could be in the same family! Weird, huh? I often wonder if my sister and I begged Heavenly Father to let us share our mortal experience so He sent us to earth as twins.

Age
Author Unknown

Age is a quality of mind;
If you have left your dreams behind,
If hope is cold,
If you no longer look ahead,
If your ambition's fires are dead,
Then you are old.
But if from life you take the best,
If in life you keep the zest,
If love you hold,
No matter how the years go by,
No matter how the birthdays fly,
You are not old.

I also like the quote by Samuel Ullman: "Years may wrinkle the skin, but to give up enthusiasm wrinkles the soul." Always be working on a new dream. Write a list of fifty things you want to do in your life. I'm not even that old and already I've checked a bunch off my list. Of course, I've taken a few items off my list that I had originally thought I wanted to do, like climb Mount Everest. It's just too doggone cold up there!

Knowledge is basically an accumulation of facts. Wisdom is the correct application of that knowledge. Douglas Adams said, "Human beings, who are almost unique in having the ability to learn from the experience of others, are also remarkable for their apparent disinclination to do so."

There is a story about an old man dying in the hospital and his wife, Ethyl, is lovingly sitting at his side. She tenderly holds his hand while he reflects upon their life together. "Ethyl," he begins his last words of farwell, "the first year of our marriage we worked really hard, but we still lost half our farm. You were always by my side, Ethyl." He continued, "The second year of our marriage we worked even harder, and we still lost the other half of the farm, but you were always by my side, Ethyl. We had five businesses. They all went under, but you were always by my side, Ethyl. We had eleven kids and couldn't afford to educate them, but you were always by my side, Ethyl. After all these years, I've decided you're bad luck, Ethyl!"

Here's the deal: this is *your* life. If your life is boring, whose fault is that? Yours. Don't blame others for everything. Take control of your life. Fill it with experiences that will enrich your mortal life, teach you things that will make you more Christlike, and bring joy to yourself and others.

Don't fix the blame; fix the problem! You have one shot at life and this is it. You'll waste way too much time being unhappy if you point your finger at anyone other than yourself when things go wrong. You always have a choice on how you will react. For example, if you're in a car accident that leaves your vehicle with a big dent in the side, how will you react?

- Blame the other guy and get revenge by suing him.
- Get mad, and whine and complain for weeks.
- Get depressed and convince yourself, "I'm so stupid."
- Calmly file a police report and call your insurance company.
- Be grateful you weren't hurt and say, "Boy, am I lucky!"

Have you ever been around someone who is super cranky and complains all the time? Hopefully, that isn't you! Negative people can really pull you down. Surround yourself with people who inspire and uplift you. People will surround *you* when you're the one who is cheerful, motivating, and inspiring.

When things are bad, remember: it won't always be this way. Take one day at a time. When things are good, remember: it won't always be this way. Enjoy every great moment.

Old Granny Glasses

Much of what happens to us in later years depends on the preparation we made in earlier years. Good preparation might include:

* Practicing good health habits so we can live as long as possible and be productive and active as long as possible. Are you focusing on the don'ts in the Word of Wisdom or the do's for healthy eating? An ancient Chinese saying is, "He who does not have time for his health today will not have health for his time tomorrow." My husband used to go to the gym to work out. Now he goes and calls it "age therapy."
* Living within our means and saving for the times when our earnings cease.
* Developing positive attitudes about the elderly and learning to value their wisdom and experience.
* Cultivating a desire to serve others in ways that are not possible when a full-time occupation demands attention.
* Learning new skills so that we can do some of the things we always wanted to do but never had time for.

Why is it that some of the best quotes and poems are written by "anonymous"? If I wrote something really inspiring, I'd want everyone to know it! (wink) Here's a well-known list of truths learned about life:

* I've learned that we don't have to change friends if we understand that friends change.
* I've learned that no matter how good friends are, they're going to hurt you every once in a while and you must forgive them for that.
* I've learned that sometimes the people you expect to kick you when you're down are the ones to help you get back up.
* I've learned that true friendship continues to grow, even over the longest distance. Same goes for true love.
* I've learned that just because people don't love you the way you want them to doesn't mean they don't love you with all they have.
* I've learned that maturity has more to do with what types of experiences you've had and what you've learned from them, and less to do with how many birthdays you've celebrated.
* I've learned that you cannot make people love you. All you can do is be someone who can be loved. The rest is up to them.
* I've learned that I have the right to be angry, but that doesn't give me the right to be cruel.

- ✳ I've learned that you should never tell a child that their dreams are unlikely or outlandish.
- ✳ I've learned that it isn't always enough to be forgiven by others. Sometimes you have to learn to forgive yourself.
- ✳ I've learned that no matter how bad your heart is broken, the world doesn't stop for your grief.
- ✳ I've learned that our background and circumstances may influence who we are, but we are responsible for who we become.
- ✳ I've learned that just because two people argue, that doesn't mean they don't love each other.
- ✳ I've learned that you shouldn't be so eager to find out a secret. It could change your life forever.
- ✳ I've learned that two people can look at the exact same thing and see something totally different.
- ✳ I've learned that no matter how you try to protect your children, they will eventually get hurt.
- ✳ I've learned that your life can be changed in a matter of hours by people who don't even know you.
- ✳ I've learned that even when you think you have no more to give, if a friend cries out to you, you will find the strength to help.
- ✳ I've learned that credentials on the wall do not make you a decent person.

What great truths have you learned so far? Are you writing in your journal about the lessons you're learning in life?

Write down what you know about these topics:

God:

Family:

My country:

Friendship:

Trials:

Education:

Love:

My life's purpose:

None of us knows how long our adventures on earth will last. Life is a journey, not a destination. In Doctrine and Covenants 14:7 we are counseled, "And, if you keep my commandments and endure to the end you shall have eternal life, which gift is the greatest of all the gifts of God." The word *eternal* means forever, but it also refers to the kind of life we can have—one with our Heavenly Father. What exactly does it mean to endure to the end? Endure what, and how? And when is the end? Most of us associate the word *endure* with suffering for a long time. Sounds like fun. Usually the scriptures use the term *endure* to mean to last, continue, or remain, especially pertaining to one's covenants with Christ.

Enduring to the end means being faithful to the covenants you made at baptism and in the temple. It means you keep your promises with the Lord throughout your life, no matter what. It means you don't quit when life gets tough or when those covenants become inconvenient. Can the Lord trust you with your promises? If you pay your tithing every week or month or year, that's great. But if you stop paying your tithing when you're, say, sixty-five, then it's almost as if all those years didn't count because you've stopped being faithful and enduring to the end. Don't quit—be good!

How will you spend eternity? In the smoking or non-smoking section? Get it? (Hell is hot!) Put on your eternal-vision glasses and keep enduring to the end. What are eternal-vision glasses? Seriously? Haven't you been reading this book?

FUN PARENT TRICK

When your parents aren't looking, change the background on their cell phones or computer monitors to a funny picture that will make them laugh and feel young again. They'll love you for it. Because they're so "ancient," you'll probably have to teach them how to do that little technology trick.

FOR THE GUYS' EYES ONLY

If you ever want to know what a girl's mind feels like, imagine an Internet browser with 2,857 tabs open. All. The. Time. Girls have a really good memories too, so don't get them mad. They'll remember what you did forever. Their brains are like filing cabinets where they store away information and can easily retrieve something you did or said years ago. I'm just saying. This is your fair warning.

For the Lasses with Glasses

Girls worry about aging and wrinkles. Of course, at your age you feel invincible and can't imagine getting old. Unfortunately, it's going to happen. The trick is to age with grace.

Audrey Hepburn is one of the classic beauties of the ages. She was a famous movie star in the '50s and later became the spokesperson for the United Nations Children's Fund. She often quoted *Time Tested Beauty Tips* by Sam Levenson:

> For attractive lips, speak words of kindness.
> For lovely eyes, seek out the good in people.
> For a slim figure, share your food with the hungry.
> For beautiful hair, let a child run his or her fingers through it once a day.
> For poise, walk with the knowledge that you never walk alone.

. . . .

> The beauty of a woman is not in the clothes she wears, the figure she carries, or the way she combs her hair. The beauty of a woman must be seen from in her eyes, because that is the doorway to her heart, the place where love resides.
>
> The beauty of a woman is not in a facial mode, but the true beauty in a woman is reflected in her soul. It is the caring that she lovingly gives and the passion that she shows. The beauty of a woman with passing years only grows.

RANDOM JOKE ABOUT GLASSES

Where is the eye located?
—Between the H and the J.

SUCCESS TIPS FROM MY FRIENDS WHO ARE SMART TEENS AND ADULTS

* Life is ten percent what happens to you and ninety percent how you react. Make the best of what you've been given. —Hailey Sheridan (I've known her since she was born. She just got married to a wonderful guy, and I'm so happy for her. The older she gets, the more she looks like her beautiful mother, a friend I've known since college. It seems like just a few minutes ago.)
* Serve others. —Rebecca Cornish Talley (She is another author friend of mine who certainly practices what she preaches. She volunteers countless hours helping LDS authors who are members of our author group at www.ldstorymakers.com. Every year we host a terrific writer's conference for anyone who has the itch to write and learn more about the industry. You can see her books at www.rebeccatalley.com.)
* Dream as if you'll live forever. Live as if you'll die today. —James Dean (No, I didn't know him. He died long before I was born. I'm not *that* old! He was a famous movie star in the '50s.)

CHAPTER TWENTY

Google Glasses: Being a Part of the Future

Elder M. Russell Ballard spoke to BYU–Hawaii students several years ago and said, "This is your world, the world of the future, with inventions undreamed of that will come in your lifetime as they have in mine. How will you use these inventions? More to the point, how will you use them to further the work of the Lord?" (*Commencement Address*, 15 Dec. 2007)

Do you blog? Do you tweet? Do you have Pinterest boards? Do you have an Instagram account? Snapchat? Tumblr? What am I thinking? You're under twenty so of course you do! There are so many fun things you can do on those spaces. Did you ever think that they are tools that can be used to help build the Lord's kingdom? Of course they are! Do you use them for that?

The thing about the Internet is that once you post something, it's there *forever*. Even delete buttons don't really make things go away. Did you know that? Be careful what you share with the world. Before you post anything, remember that your parents, future employers, future college admission teams, potential Church investigators may run across your words and images. Don't be spontaneous, but take a few seconds to truly think about what you're sharing might say about you and your values.

Google Glasses

Randall L. Ridd, the Second Counselor in the Young Men General Presidency, gave a fantastic talk at the April 2014 general conference about technology. He said, "Owning a smartphone does not make you smart, but using it wisely can" ("The Choice Generation"). People are always watching you. You are the only Book of Mormon some people will ever read.

The leaders of the Church have encouraged us to "get out there" and be a part of the world's discussions. Be careful not to be preachy though. Even good people can be turned off by that. Many of us have jumped in and found ourselves drowning in unpleasant debates with friends we adore. It's frightening to receive comments from friends who suddenly attack our values, especially when it comes to political and religious discussions. It hurts too. Be kind if you disagree with someone. Remember that the Spirit cannot dwell where there is contention.

Deirdra Eden, author of *The Watchers*, said, "Strength isn't always about weapons, armor and fighting skills. Strength is also about learning to control what is inside you." Never post a comment in anger. It will make you look as hostile as the person who wants to argue. You *will* regret it. If you post something about the Church and someone tries to make you look stupid or says something cruel about your beliefs, what should you say? Here are a few suggestions on how you could reply:

- Say nothing. They're probably dying to see how you're going to react. If you don't respond, it can often diffuse the situation. Depending on the social media you're using, you might be able to delete their comment.
- "We can disagree and still be friends."
- "I value our friendship, so please don't put down my values."
- "Are you sure you really want to write that on my page for everyone to see?"
- "I'm disappointed in you."
- "Choose carefully what you post because it reveals who you really are."

Whether you want to or not, you influence others . . . for good or for bad. Take it upon yourself to add some class to your school. My third son (the one on his mission in Nicaragua right now) is super social and fun. During his junior year in high school, he decided to declare a "Suit Up Day" at school and convinced all of his "bros" to dress up. Now, Mormons are used to wearing suits, but none of his friends were. It was kind of a big deal for them. Needless to say, it created quite a stir at school. All of the girls were impressed. (That let be a lesson to you, guys.) It was such a hit that they had a few more "Suit Up" days at school before he graduated. The bottom line is that people watch you to see what a "real" Mormon is like.

Do you know what the two most popular searched topics on the Internet are?

- Pornography
- Genealogy

Don't you think that's interesting? Don't you think it's also a bit obvious that one is Satan's trap and the other is the Lord's work? We are so lucky to live during this time in the world's history. Our ancestors had to hunt for days for their food. We just have to wait for minutes in front of a microwave. My kids call that "First World Problems." Our ancestors spent the majority of their time just tending to basic necessities, but we can clothe, feed, and care for ourselves in mere minutes. So, what are you doing with all of that extra time? I would imagine that the Lord expects more of us because we simply have more time. Are you helping to build His kingdom or are you spending endless hours building Minecraft?

Can you even imagine all of the cool advances in technology that you're going to see in your lifetime? You live in such an exciting time in history! Your future is so bright!

Write down some ways you can gently share gospel principles on any of these accounts you have:

Facebook:

Instagram:

Twitter:

Pinterest:

Goodreads:

Snapchat:

Blog:

YouTube channel:

Tumblr:

Digg:

Google+:

Texting:

FOR THE GUYS' EYES ONLY

Here's a quick "broment" for you guys. Before this book ends, I have to tell you about my oldest son. He's twenty-five years old and completely awesome. He's like Captain Moroni in every way. Needless to say, I'm one proud mama. He is pretty shy and quiet by nature, but he has forced himself to go outside of his comfort zone. Because of his willingness to push himself, he has been able to do some pretty amazing things. He served a mission in Argentina and graduated from BYU, where he was captain of the Army Ranger team in the ROTC program there. He was recently commissioned as an officer, after getting paid to jump out of airplanes in Airborne school and translate Spanish for Army dentists in El Salvador. He won a couple grand at a marksmanship competition and received a prestigious award from a two-star general for winning first place in several physical fitness competitions. See, I told you he was awesome.

Did any of that come easy to him? Absolutely not. Remember, he is a really shy guy and had to work hard and push himself. His motivation came from within, not from nagging parents. I asked him what advice he had for you and this is what he said, "Take a shot, even when you don't think you'll make it. A lot of the coolest things I've done (working with Army Green Berets, doing an internship for a secretive government agency, dating beautiful girls) were things I didn't think I had a shot at, but I tried anyway and made it. You'll always regret not trying, so go for it!"

For the Lasses with Glasses

Girls are especially interested in social media. We can't help it. We love to talk and share and talk some more! Just be careful not to "over-share." You know what I mean, right? You probably know that one girl who has to post a picture of the sandwich she just ate and every other detail of her life every hour. Hopefully, you're not that girl.

I have a young friend who posts about a million "selfies" every day. Here's the painful truth: you are *not* the center of the universe. I'm sure you're super fascinating, but just pace yourself on how often you post about yourself. Instead, include pictures of other people, things that inspire you, and things that you think will bless others. People will "follow" you when they feel their life is being enriched because of what you share.

RANDOM JOKE ABOUT GLASSES

Patient: I always see spots before my eyes.
Optician: Didn't the new glasses help?
Patient: Sure, now I see the spots more clearly.

SUCCESS TIPS FROM MY FRIENDS WHO ARE WISE

* Eating solely the Frisbee-sized peanut butter cookies from the cafeteria and drinking diet sodas with your lunch money every day isn't the best fuel choice for your body. —Karen Oliver Sampson (She is a dear friend of mine from high school whom I always admired for her many talents. She just won an award for being an awesome elementary school teacher in Arizona. It's so much fun to grow up and see your friends go on to bless other people's lives like that!)
* Often we look for a magic secret or new technique that will produce tremendous returns and results. Those seeking this will never find it—for the secret to success is to continually live and apply basic, simple fundamentals over a long period of time. —Cameron C. Taylor (He is an author who has written some scholarly books about the gospel, finances, and America. His newest book is called *8 Attributes of Great Achievers* and is full of success tips like the one he wanted to share with you in my book. Check him out at www.CameronCTaylor.com.)
* I've always been inspired by Helen Keller, who said, "Keep your face toward the sunshine and you cannot see the shadows." —Cheri Crane
* Walk your talk. Actions speak louder than words. —Paula Rice Rogers (Paula is my wonderful aunt. She was a high-powered businesswoman for many years, but always kept focused on her family and the Savior as the most important in her life. What a great example and blessing she has been to so many people. Be sure to surround yourself with inspiring people!)

CHAPTER TWENTY-ONE

"Songlasses": Your Future with Him Is So Bright!

This final chapter is all about "Songlasses!" The Son, of course, refers to Jesus Christ because He is the Light of the World! Your future is very bright, especially when you use His light to guide you through it. How do you feel about Jesus Christ?

Write your thoughts about Him here:

When I was on my mission in Spain, we would go to the parks in the early evenings when Spaniards take strolls with their families. We would set up these tall sandwich board poster thingies with pictures of the plan of happiness and the Restoration of the gospel on them. We called them "pancartas." My job was to hunt down people and strike up a conversation with the goal of inviting them back to the pancartas to learn more about the gospel. I thought it was really fun to try to catch the attention of people as they walked by. When I found interested people, I would walk them over to the pancartas and let the other missionaries continue the discussion. Then I would run off to find more.

One approach I often used to start a conversation with people was to ask them to answer some questions in a survey I was doing. (Remember that idea from the dating chapter?) Here are the five questions I would use.

- Do you believe in God?
- Do you believe He spoke anciently with prophets?
- Do you believe God changes, or is He always the same?
- If you believe in God and that He spoke with prophets before and that He never changes, then is it possible that He could speak to prophets today?
- If there were one of God's prophets on the earth today, would you want to know it and hear what he has to say?

I thought it was fascinating to see the lightbulb turn on in people's minds when they followed that logic and honestly reflected on their answers. What were *your* answers?

Sister Bonnie L. Oscarson, Young Women General President, gave a great talk in the October 2013 general conference. She taught,

> True conversion is more than merely having a knowledge of gospel principles and implies even more than just having a testimony of those principles. It is possible to have a testimony of the gospel without living it. Being truly converted means we are acting upon what we believe and allowing it to create "a mighty change in us, or in our hearts." In the booklet *True to the Faith*, we learn that "conversion is a process, not an event. You become converted as a result of . . . righteous efforts to follow the Savior." It takes time, effort, and work. . . .
>
> We have to go through that same process if we want to gain that same kind of commitment. The Savior taught, "If any man will do his will, he shall know of the doctrine, whether it be of God, or whether I speak of myself." ("Be Ye Converted," *Ensign*, Nov. 2013)

Sometimes we say we'll have a testimony about tithing, for example, after we see the blessing and before we pay. What? The prophet Moroni in the Book of Mormon wrote, "I would show unto the world that faith is things which are hoped for and not seen; wherefore, dispute not because ye see not, for *ye receive no witness until after the trial of your faith*" (Ether 12:6; italics added).

No matter how inspired your parents and youth leaders may be, you are responsible for your own conversion. No one can be converted for you, and no one can force you to be converted. I know that God is real, but you have to find out for yourself. Don't treat that search lightly. The answer will make all the difference in your life.

My husband is a convert to the Church. How did Tom Boice become a Mormon? Well, I'll tell you. Here is his story in his own words about how he found out what he really believed.

> Growing up in the Presbyterian Church meant that some time in my high school years I was supposed to take a confirmation course before officially becoming a member of the church. The course was once a week in the evening. I only made it through one class. I was a senior in high school.
>
> The teacher was a guy in his thirties and he had a manual he used for the course. There were about twenty or so high school kids in the class and we were being instructed on the church's doctrine point by point. While he was going over the Holy Trinity one of the kids raised his hand and asked, "How do we know that's true?"
>
> "What?"
>
> "How do we know that this thing about God, Jesus, and the Holy Ghost being different manifestations of one God is really how it is?"
>
> "We have it written here in the manual about the Nicene Creed that this is the true nature of God."
>
> "Yeah, but how do we know that's really how it is? Couldn't they be three separate beings or something like that?"
>
> "I'm telling you, that's how it is! If you don't want to believe it, then you shouldn't be in this church because this is what we believe!"
>
> The kid didn't ask any more questions and I didn't go to any more classes.
>
> About this time, my best friend was Glenn Allen. His family lived in the house behind ours and we used to climb over the wall to goof around. Besides playing sports together, we used to have some interesting philosophical discussions. That's how I started learning about the Church. The idea of a book of scripture chronicling prophets on the American continent seemed a bit far-fetched but not completely impossible. I had a reasonably open mind. I think I would have done pretty much anything the Lord wanted me to do and believed whatever the Lord wanted me to believe, even the Book

of Mormon if I knew it was from the Lord Jesus Christ. But therein lies the problem—how do you really know?

Glenn had a lot of things already figured out. He was going to graduate from high school, go to BYU, go on a mission, get married, have a family, and live happily ever after. The idea of going away for two years to teach people about his religion was remarkable to me, but it was not something I would have considered doing. Glenn actually had the exact mission where he wanted to go figured out: New Zealand. Of course, you don't get to pick your mission and no one ever seems to get their first choice, but for some reason, that was where Glenn dreamed of going on his mission and he just knew he'd go there.

Near the end of the school year, Glenn asked me if I wanted to go to a seminary graduation party at some LDS member's house. My reaction was, "No, thanks. I didn't even go seminary much less graduate from it."

"It's just a party, Tom. It'll be fun. They have a pool at this house and a bunch of other fun things to do."

"No really, it's not my group. I'm not even a Mormon."

"Come on, Tom."

"No, thanks, Glenn."

"My sister Robin is going to be there."

"Okay, where and what time?" (I thought she was a babe.)

He clearly knew how to motivate me. We went to the pool party, each with a different agenda. Glen wanted me to be around Church members who would fellowship me, and I just wanted to hang around Robin. Well, it turned out that Robin had a new boyfriend, so I got nowhere with my goal, but while I was at the home, an interesting thing happened. I noticed a unique picture on the wall in the hallway.

It was a painting of an old guy from some ancient culture praying in the woods next to a hole in the ground. He was kneeling in the snow and his hands were clasped on some plates that looked like they were made out of gold. His eyes were shut, but his head was tilted heavenward. Below the painting was a quote:

"And when ye shall receive these things, I would exhort you that ye would ask God, the Eternal Father, in the name of Christ, if these things are not true; and if ye shall ask with a sincere heart, with real intent, having faith in Christ, he will manifest the truth of it unto you by the power of the Holy Ghost. And by the power of the Holy Ghost ye may know the truth of all things" (Moroni 10:4–5).

I didn't know where that statement came from, but it was an epiphany for me. This was the level of assurance I would require before joining any church. God would need to let me know it was true. If He did it through the power of the Holy Ghost, that was fine with me. That stayed on my mind for a long time.

"Sonqlasses"

At the end of our first year at different colleges, Glenn came back to spend the summer with his family and wait for his mission call. One day as we drove up to Glenn's house after a day at the beach, there was a gigantic 4 x 8 plywood sign on his front yard. The spray paint on the sign said simply, "New Zealand!" His mission call had come in the mail and his mother just couldn't resist opening the letter.

I'm sure Glenn wanted me to join the Church before he left on his mission, but I wasn't going to commit until I had a fulfillment of Moroni's promise. I did a lot of reading and praying, but the Church needed to be more than something that made sense and sounded good. I wanted revelation. I learned that fasting could help bring answers to prayer, so I tried that. I didn't want to tell people I was fasting because you're not supposed to do it to be "seen of men," so at dinner time I would tell my mom I wasn't hungry or make some kind of excuse not to eat. My parents were probably worried about me, especially in light of how much food I normally consumed.

I still wasn't getting my answer so I figured I would go longer than twenty-four hours on my fast, like maybe forty-eight or however long it took to get an answer. That was a challenge because I was working at a restaurant two or three nights a week and would always get a free meal during my break. On the second day of one of those fasts, I was getting so weak and hungry that I finally broke down. I only made it thirty-six hours, but I think the Lord gave me some credit for lasting that long. If you knew how much food I normally ate, you'd have more respect for the effort.

Glenn was disappointed that I hadn't joined the Church yet, but he was very excited about going to New Zealand. When he learned that he had visa problems and would not be able to go to New Zealand immediately, he was frustrated. Surprisingly, Glenn's temporary assignment was a mission in California, super close to where we grew up! At this point, I was back at school in California and living in the dorm when Glenn called me. He was serving about twenty-four miles from his parents' home, about twenty-eight miles from where I was going to school. Weird, huh? You never go on a mission that close to home. You're not supposed to call your friends on your mission either, but I guess he looked at it like I was an investigator and he could call me to make sure I was still praying and reading.

Several weeks went by, and he would call about once a week and we would talk for a few minutes. He'd tell me there was still no word on his visa or even why it was being held up, and serving in California was okay, but he really wanted to get to New Zealand, which is where he felt he was supposed to be. One day Glenn's call was different. He said, "Tom, I've been praying about this a lot, trying to get the answer to why I'm not in New Zealand and why my visa is being held up. I feel like I have work to do in New Zealand

and I'm not being allowed to do my job. Anyway, I finally got a clear answer. In fact, it's like I heard a voice answering my prayer. Not like a voice I heard with my ear, but a voice I heard in my heart. So, you want to know what the answer is?"

"Sure."

"There's a job to do here that I haven't finished yet."

"Uh-huh."

"So, Tom, can you think of what that job might be?"

"Okay, I'll keep praying and asking, but I'm not going to join the Church unless I get an answer."

"Okay, but could you please hurry up and get an answer, because I really want to go to New Zealand."

I spent a lot of time on my knees. The desire to know, by the Spirit, whether this was right had grown very intense. It was time. I'd done the reading. I'd done the fasting. I was living a clean life. I felt like I was honest in heart and was willing to live up to the Lord's expectations, whatever the answer was. Just give me an answer and I'll act on it, but I need an answer of some kind. And, Lord, make it quick so Glenn can get to New Zealand!

Well, I got an answer. It's hard to explain how intensely I felt it. I was praying and listening for an answer, and suddenly something changed. I had this assurance come to me. Not something I decided, but a feeling that was given to me from a source other than myself. A knowledge was being given to me, not by any of my five senses but a spiritual assurance that I knew was being provided by the Lord. It went beyond, "I think this is the right thing." It was more like, "Yes, this is true. This is right and you have your witness." At that moment I knew I should be baptized as a member of the Church.

Monday afternoon, after I finished my classes, I called Glenn to tell him what happened. He was overjoyed. His first baptism on his mission was going to be his best friend! How many new missionaries get to do that? As soon as we hung up the phone, Glenn's phone rang. He picked the phone back up and heard, "Elder, your visa just came through and we have you scheduled for a flight this Saturday afternoon." Glenn called me right back to tell me and I didn't believe him. So he put three other elders on the line and they confirmed that he had gotten the call as soon as we had finished talking. Glenn hadn't even taken his hand off the phone before it rang. I was baptized by my best friend and then he jumped on a plane and flew off to finish his mission in New Zealand!

What's interesting is that there is a phrase in Glenn's patriarchal blessing that talks about how he will teach and baptize people both near and far. I was the "near" one, and you can't get much farther than New Zealand. I know the Book of Mormon and the Church are true, not because it feels good to believe those things but because God told me!"

"Songlasses"

My husband later went on to serve his own mission and continues to share the gospel with others. He has been a wonderful husband and father. He now thinks I'm more of a babe than Glenn's sister.

In the beginning of the Book of Mormon, we learn that there were two different sets of plates: one for the historical events and one for more spiritual experiences. Have you ever considered doing that too?

Wouldn't it be awesome to read a spiritual diary written by your parents or grandparents? Create a special place where you record your spiritual experiences that build your testimony and it can strengthen the testimony of your descendants. Generations yet unborn may read your words and be led closer to the Savior! You can call it your spiritual journal. When I notice that there are long gaps in time between the entries in my spiritual journal, it reminds me that I need to be continuously working on strengthening and building my testimony.

Look for miracles in your everyday life. Every week I get quite a few letters from my friends who are serving missions all over the world. Each letter includes mention of the miracles that were observed during the past week. *Every* letter includes sweet, touching testimonies about how the Lord's hand has touched their efforts. Missionaries are being taught to **LOOK** for those miracles. What's even more important is that they are **SEEING** miracles. Everywhere. Open your eyes. They're all around you too.

We've spent this entire book talking about vision. May you **SEE** yourself, others, and the world through the Savior's loving eyes. More important, may He **SEE** you in His.

Your future is so *bright*!

RANDOM JOKE ABOUT GLASSES

Optician: You need glasses.
Patient: But I'm wearing glasses.
Optician: Then I need glasses.

SUCCESS TIPS FROM MY FRIENDS WHO ARE SMART TEENS AND ADULTS

* Don't be afraid of your dreams because of the time it will take to accomplish them. The time will pass anyway, whether you work towards your dreams or not, so you might as well be making daily progress on them! —Brad Boice (He's my third son and currently serving his mission in Nicaragua! He's a break-dancer and super fun to be around. Hey, girls, he'll be available in two years!)
* Set your goals to a high standard and never give up. —Antonio Roman Reyna (He's a friend of mine who was a two-time Golden Glove

Champion in Nevada and an Army Ranger in the Special Forces. Talk about discipline, eh?)

* Be true to yourself. Be who you are. Love yourself. —Shara Edwards
* Believe in yourself. If you don't, then no one else will either. —Sheila Windley Staley
* Surround yourself with positive people and distance yourself from negative people. If you're negative, change that mindset as it only hinders you. —Nathan Grant
* Your future is *so* bright! —Trina Boice (Me!)

Be sure to check out the fun website that was created especially for this book and for *you*! It features pictures of LDS teens from all over the world, fun videos, and more! Go to my website www.trinaboice.com to find the link.

About the Author

Trina Boice grew up in California, but she currently lives in Las Vegas, Nevada. She teaches classes at the famous Le Cordon Bleu School for Culinary Arts as well as for BYU–Idaho online. In 2004 she was honored as the California Young Mother of the Year, an award which completely amuses her four sons. She earned two bachelor's degrees from BYU where she competed on the speech and debate team and the ballroom dance team. She was president of the National Honor Society Phi Eta Sigma and served as ASBYU Secretary of Student Community Services.

Trina also studied at the University of Salamanca in Spain and later returned there to serve an LDS mission in Madrid for a year and a half. She has a real estate license, travel agent license, two master's degrees, and a black belt in Tae Kwon Do, though she's the first to admit that she'd pass out from fright if she were ever really attacked by a bad guy.

She worked as a legislative assistant for a congressman in Washington DC and was given the Points of Light Award and Presidential Volunteer Service Award for her domestic and international community service. She wrote a column called "The Boice Box" for a newspaper in Georgia, where she lived for fifteen years. She taught Spanish at a private high school and ran an appraisal business with her husband for twenty years. She currently writes for several websites and is the Entertainment News Editor for *Bella Online*. Check out her movie reviews at www.MovieReviewMaven.blogspot.com

Trina was selected by KPBS in San Diego to be a political correspondent during the last presidential election. If she told you what she really did, she'd have to kill you.

A popular and entertaining speaker, Trina is the author of seventeen books, with another one hitting stores soon. You can read more about her books and upcoming events at www.trinaboice.com.

About the Illustrator

Brittany Long is the oldest of six children and was raised in Las Vegas, Nevada. Her favorite pastime has always been reading. She graduated with a BA in English from Southern Utah University, where she focused her study on creative writing and illustration. In late 2008, Brittany first began writing and drawing daily autobiographical comics, and she hasn't missed a day since. She recently returned from a full-time mission in Japan. She also enjoys baking and eating pies, playing the piano, and hanging out with dogs. You can find her daily comics at http://comicdiaries.com.